I REMEMBER

Indianapolis Youth Write about Their Lives

2019

Copyright © 2019 by INwords / Indiana Writers Center
All rights reserved.
I Remember: Indianapolis Youth Write about Their Lives: 2019
ISBN: 978-1-7324993-0-0
INwords Publications, Indianapolis, IN
Printed in the United States of America

I REMEMBER
Indianapolis Youth Write about Their Lives
2019

Edited by Darolyn "Lyn" Jones

Design by Andrea Boucher & Eileen Porzuczek

INwords Publications
1125 Brookside Avenue, Suite B25
Indianapolis, IN 46202

Student Editors: Devon Legman, Maria Piazzo, Eileen Porzuczek, & Emily Turner

Indiana Writers Center "Building a Rainbow" Youth Public Memoir Program
Executive Director Indiana Writers Center
Rachel Sahaidachny

Writer in Residence
Barbara Shoup

Education Outreach Director
Darolyn "Lyn" Jones

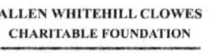

TABLE OF CONTENTS

Summer Program Overview 12

SAINT FLORIAN YOUTH LEADERSHIP AND DEVELOPMENT CENTER

JUNIOR & CORE CADETS

A'na C. 20
Aali C. 21
Adrian D. 21
Adrian L. 22
Aiden B. 22
Alijah E. 23
Alisha C. 23
Alyssa H. 24
Amauri M. 25
Amiia B. 25
Antonio S. 26
Aniyah L. 27
Anyla S. 28
Blair A. 29
Brendon M. 29
Brian R. 30
Brielle K. 30
Brylen S. 31
Bryson I. 31
Bryson W. 32
Caden D. 33
Carson S. 34

Christian S. 34

Christopher H. 35

Colton A. 35

Da'Laysia G. 36

Danae'sha R. 37

Darien W. 37

Darion S. 38

Edosa E. 39

Emery W. 40

Counselor Erica. 40

Ethan M. 41

Graham "Otis" A. 41

Graham A. 42

Issac J. 42

Isaiah J. 43

Isaiah B. 43

Israel C. 44

Ja'Lan K. 44

Jada K. 45

James G. 45

Jarin P. 46

Jason S. 46

Jathen T. 47

Jayden J. 48

Jeffery A. 48

Jeremiah K. 49

Jeremiah O. 49

Jermaine W. 50

Jordan T. 50

Joseph A. 51

Josiah T. 51

Juliana M. 51

Kaiden S.	52
Kailey P.	52
Landon H.	54
Layla W.	54
LeiLani R.	55
Lexi A.	55
Madison S.	56
Makail M.	56
Marcel M.	58
Maya B.	58
Mianna S.	59
Pharaoh P.	59
Pheldon M.	60
Preslie-Jai A.	61
Quanell C.	61
Raven R.	62
Saniia F.	62
Sevan W.	63
Skylar B.	65
Sonnie T.	65
Taryn J.	66
Taylor J.	66
Tazae H.	67
Troy W.	67
Uriah T.	67
Weston F.	68
Xavier	68
Zaiya M.	69
Zarriah M.	70
Zayden C.	71
Zayla P.	71
Zion S.	72

Zuri J. 72

CASH CLUB

Anton T. 75
DeCaya R. 76
DeMoni R. 77
Duane P. 77
Elyjah M. 78
Joniece L. 78
Jordan J. 79
Malena P. 80
Sydney B. 81
Counselor Nikki 82
Counselor Brandon 83

HORIZONS AT SAINT RICHARD'S EPISCOPAL SCHOOL

Alaya L. 87
Brooklyn T. 87
Cecila H. 87
Christian A. 88
Day'lee T. 89
Devin R. 90
Donavin C. 90
Ezra M. 91
Gyani H. 92
Harlem T. 93
Jahmir D. 93
Jamia A. 94
Jasohn S 95
Jeremiah T. 96
Jessyca C. 96

Jonathan C. 97
Joseph C. 97
Kameron J. 98
Kassidy B. 98
Kendall S. 99
Kyle M. 99
Lauryn J. 100
Ma'at D. 100
Maleik A. 101
Marcus C. 101
Ny'Asia A. 103
Paris P. 103
Quinnija T. 104
Quintarius T. 104
Romeo C. 105
Summer O. 106
Sydney S 107
Thomas M. 108
Ulysses L. 109
Zaniah W. 110

WESTMINSTER YOUTH SERVICES SUMMER PROGRAM

Alex W. 118
Angel H. 118
Ava K. 118
Breayre P. 119
Cristina B. 119
Dalilah C. 120
David A. 120
De'niyah J. 121

De'lilah J. 121
De'mone S. 122
De'lijah J. 122
Doran P 123
Elijah W. 123
Gustavo H. 124
Hayven B. 124
Jacobi N. 125
Jada F 126
James L. 126
Jayden. 127
Keiyon S. 127
Kinesha P. 128
Lindsey C. 128
Major F. 129
Mykell J. 130
Natalia F. 131
Navaeh. 131
Obiora. 132
Randall F. 132
Richard G. 133
Samarei M. 133
Samya R. 134
Sainya R. 134
Shelia G. 135
Stephan B 135
Toniah M. 136
Troy T. 136
Tyiana M 136
Zoey S. 137
Zyllah L. 137

APPENDICES

Writing Prompts	139
Editor and Designer Biographies	144
Acknowledgments	146

SUMMER PROGRAM OVERVIEW

Funded by the Summer Youth Program Fund (SYPF), as well as generous individual donors, the Indiana Writers Center's "Building a Rainbow" creative writing program serves a diverse group of more than 200 young people in Indianapolis, improving their writing and literacy skills through a series of creative writing exercises that teach them how to write the stories of their own lives. The program is named after a colorful, whimsical poster of a half-made rainbow that is covered with tiny stick figures painting, hammering and operating cranes as they work to finish it. The image is a visual reminder that there are many small steps in creating something beautiful—a piece of writing, a dream a goal, a life.
Working one-on-one, IWC instructors, student interns, and volunteers help the young writers get their words on the page and also encourage them to reflect upon the experiences they've written about, considering how what they've learned can help them make their dreams come true.

Writing isn't easy for anyone. Even published writers need encouragement from those who believe in them, as well as help and inspiration from fellow writers on the path. I love to sit down with a young writer who's having trouble getting started on the prompt and tease out a story by asking questions. What's the first thing that happened? Where were you? Who else was there? What were you wearing? What did you do when it happened? Say? What did others do or say? How did you feel? How did you show that feeling? If you didn't show the feeling, what was it like kept inside you—a fire, a dull pain in your heart, a rocket about to burst into the air?

Sometimes students heave a great sigh of boredom when the questions begin, but inevitably they start answering, almost in spite of themselves. Pretty soon, they sit up a little straighter, lean forward—and then, best tof all, they start to smile, and I know a story has come alive inside them. Which makes me smile, too, and fills me up with the most exquisite kind of joy. At this point, they usually say something that would make a good first sentence.
"Write that down," I say. Then write what happened next. And next.
They do. And, as if by magic, the begins to unspool onto the page.

I leave them, bent over the
page, writing furiously, and move on, hungry for that moment of combustion with another student. And then another.

This is happening all over the room. Each of our instructors, interns, and volunteers sit at tables and work one-on-one with students. The air is full of stories the world needs to hear.
So we collected them and put them in this book.
It was a pleasure and a privilege to work with the young people from St. Florian Youth Development Camp, Horizons at St. Richard's School, and Westminster Neighborhood Services' Summer Camp this year.
I know you will love their stories as much as I do.

—Barbara Shoup
Writer in Residence
Indiana Writers Center

○ ○ ○

COLLECTED
WRITING

○ ○ ○

SAINT FLORIAN YOUTH LEADERSHIP AND DEVELOPMENT CENTER

"All Eyes Forward!"
"Click"

Founded by two Indianapolis Firefighters in 1992, the Saint Florian Youth Leadership and Development Center provides Indianapolis youth an opportunity to develop leadership skills, problem solving methods, and survival tactics, as well as fostering core values such as honesty, respect, responsibility and character. After-school programs, tobacco-free programs, rites of passage programs, alcohol and violence prevention programs, college preparation programs, summer leadership camp, and youth ambassador programs are among the services the Saint Florian Center has provided over 30,000 youth since its inception. Saint Florian is the patron saint of firefighters.

The Saint Florian Center Youth Leadership and Development Summer Camp serves between 100-125 students each summer, ages 6-18. Over the course of seven weeks, students learn about the world around them and how to be successful in it by participating in a wide range of activities that include academics, science and technology, nonfiction writing, team-building, college campus visits, physical fitness, and art.

The Indiana Writers Center has been proudly partnering with Battalion Chief Firefighter Tony Williamson and the Saint Florian Center for nine years. When it's time to capture the attention of over hundred students—at once—we shout out, "All Eyes Forward!"

And the response from those young, strong future black leaders as they snap their heads forward and raise their hands in allegiance, is a harmonious chorus of "CLICK!"

One of the many denotative meanings of "click," is "to make a sharp sound," and more informally, "to succeed or to make a hit." These young beautiful black voices do exactly that.. They write to believe

Saint Florian

and to succeed. And by writing authentically, for real—not for school—their words, their message makes a sharp noise and hits home.

At the Indiana Writers Center, we lovingly refer to the JC's as "the littles," the Core as "the middles," and the CASH as "the bigs." Chief Firefighter Tony daily reminds his students that this camp is full of love and respect. He stresses to his young leaders that they can make a difference—they change the world. They repeat their creed daily:

I was made to lead.
Put on this Earth to see
How this world could be.

With a passion
For my followers, I will
Initiate those actions
Needing change.

Accept the risk
Of possible failure, and
shoulder the blame. I will
inspire others to follow
this creed, to be
trustworthy in my
thoughts, my words, and
my deeds.
I do all this because
I was made to LEAD!

#blacklivesmatter

We are grateful to be included in the magic and be part of what Tony calls "the love" that happens every summer at Saint Florian's Youth Leadership Camp. Every summer, we watch our littles grow into middles, our middles into bigs, and our bigs graduate and enter the world.

When we arrive on Day 1, there is a reunion rush of huggings and hellos.

"What are we going to write about this year, Miss Lyn?"

"Is Intern Alyssa coming back? Corrie? Michael?"

"Are we going to be in the book again this year?"

"Writing is my favorite part of camp!"

Imagine that… writing a favorite. How many kids say that about their English class in school? Thanks to the bigs talking with the middles and the middles talking with the littles, the students know that we at the Indiana Writers Center believe in the power of story, and believe their stories are important and should be shared with the world. They also know, like Tony and his staff at Saint Florian, that we believe in them.

We write for real, not for school. At the Indiana Writers Center, we are a community writing center, and we are a community of writers. We practice writing like real writers write. We tell stories about significant moments in our lives, we write about why black lives matter, and we give voice to our heartaches and to our hopes.

Our young leaders at Saint Florian know that the proud words they speak so loudly during Author's Chair will be published and read by family, friends, the community, and future generations. And even at age 6, they get it—they take it seriously. They understand their responsibility in sharing those important stories about their young, black lives.

It's an honor to be trusted with someone's story. JC and Core instructors Miss Lyn, Miss Emily, Miss Barb, and Cash instructor, Miss Kelsey, thank you, Saint Florian littles, middles, and bigs, for trusting us with your stories.

We chose a super hero theme for this book because we believe that the kids we work with every summer, despite facing multiple barriers — racial bias, poverty, food deserts, and underserved public and charter schools — they fight the good fights. Like Superman, they fight for truth and justice for themselves, their families, their friends, and their communities. Writer Maya Angelou says that a hero

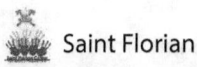 Saint Florian

is any person really intent on making this a better place for all people. Listening to what comes out of the mouths of these babes should inspire you that these children are heroes who intend to make this world a better and safer place for all. They don't wear a cape or an S on their chest. But, I assure you they are labeled. In their voice, you will hear them refuse to be labeled, but instead define themselves by their actions and in this book, their words.

Now, all eyes forward to your very bright futures, Saint Florian Cadets, because yes, you were made to lead! (And wear a cape!)

"CLICK!"

Miss Lyn

Dr. Darolyn "Lyn" Jones, Faculty Instructor and Education Outreach Director, Building a Rainbow Youth Memoir Program, Indiana Writers Center

—Miss Lyn
Dr. Darolyn "Lyn" Jones
 Faculty Instructor and Education Outreach Director
Building a Rainbow Youth Memoir Program
Indiana Writers Center

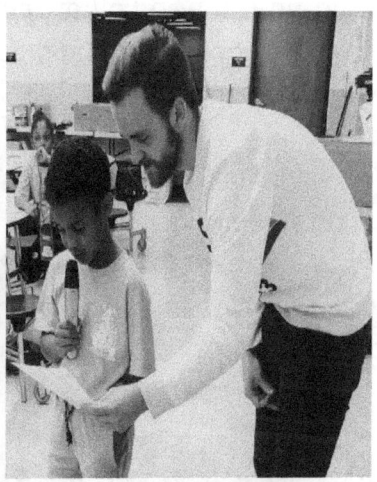

○ SAINT FLORIAN JUNIOR & CORE CADETS ○

A'na C.
age 12

My Best Effort

A time when me and other people felt proud of me is when I do good and set examples for them. Especially by getting good grades, When I'm in clubs that can help the environment, and when I help other people.

When I was in S.T.E.M. camp, it was only for girls because people always thought that girls couldn't be engineers and that girls weren't really into math or science. So they made a camp for girls to be smart and to teach them that they can do anything they put their mind to. I thought that it was such a good thing that they had done. When I get good grades, I get into more high academic class and the good grades will help me get into a good college.
When I do my best effort, it just makes people proud to see me do good. Especially when they see me do well. There are some other things I had did that made me proud like make the basketball team. I didn't make it the first year but at least I had tried, and that made me proud. Since I really had committed to trying hard this year, I feel really proud. It makes me proud when I know that people are proud of me. When I try I'm still going to be proud because I tried. Even when I learn new things, I'm proud because I can use it in life. I'm always proud of myself when I do a good deed, when no one else does.

Aali C.
age 9

Happy Tears for the Happiest Place on Earth

Since you asked I'll tell you why I'm feeling happy. So it was Christmas, and we got out Christmas pajamas on. Then my dad said he wanted to play a game. He said wherever my finger goes, we have to walk there. He led us to the backroom. When we got there we saw presents. Then we opened all of our presents. They told us to open the last one and it was a hoverboard and we asked for them for a long time. My mom got us suitcases and she said to open them it had a Disney World paper in there and they said we were going to Disney World. Then I cried with happy tears because it was my first time and we stayed for two weeks.

o o o

Adrian D.
age 13

I'm Getting Better

Have you ever felt like you never wanted to anything but stay in bed? I'm pretty sure we all have. Ever since my grandpa died on my birthday two years ago, I haven't been the same. I became more distant from the outside world besides going to school. I've had plenty of friends, even had a girlfriend. I've changed so much. Lying, stealing, all those things started to ruin my relationships with my family. Things have been starting to show in school too. I've always been an all A's and B's student, but for the first and hopefully last time I had an F. It's not like me--work was hard, but it was just I felt unmotivated. Didn't wanna go to school, didn't wanna go out to family outings, just wanna sleep in class. I totally changed, and I had given up on my future dreams. Instead spending nights listening to sad music doing what I like to call "simping." "Simping" is where you are just sad. I felt like life couldn't get any worse. This eventually ruined that relationship I had with that girlfriend. I just got insecure, and I started regretting that decision of me breaking up with her, but I got over it, well kinda. Things are still rough, but they're getting better. I'm going out more, getting out of my bed to go outside. Now all I can do is hope for the best and work on getting better.

Adrian L.
age 8

The Tragedy

Have you ever had the worst day ever? I have one of those days. Read my story, it was. One day I was riding my bike. "La La La, I'm riding my bike," I said. Oh! For those who know me. I am Adrian L. Now, we must continue the story! So, I was around the court riding my bike, when I saw a car! I was riding with only one car and then I noticed...I noticed...a car it was going down the street heading right for me. "This is the end of me," I thought. Then I heard my mom call me, "Adrian, get out of the street." So, I got back on my big bike, rode up the court in the grass as fast as I could and...When I was riding I fell down and got hurt and busted my knee. "Here comes the tragedy," I said. The End! Oh! Thanks for reading my story!

○ ○ ○

Aiden B.
age 13

Turdy Day

So, I woke up to my mom yelling at me "Get up! We're gonna be late!"

So I got up and told my mom "I'm gonna take a shower."

She said "NO TIME!" So I didn't take a shower. I got my clothes, then got my pencil, then I heard the bus, then I RAN to the bus. At the time it was winter, so as I ran and I slipped UNDER the bus. And it HURT, so I got up walked to the other side, and I got on. As I walked into school, I put my jacket into my locker and grabbed my books and school materials. I walked to science class and my day was kinda good, but lunch time comes around and long story short I got into a fight and I got grounded. No Xbox, PS4---all taken and yeah. Overall my day was TURDY.

Alijah E.
age 8

Basketball

I feel proud when my mom and dad tell me I was good, because almost all the time me and my friend always scored points. J.J. is really good at 3 pointers. One time he shot from the white line. I'm really good at 2's and layups and jump shots. When I make it, I really want to do a celebration, but my mom and dad tell me "no," because I'm playing defense and somebody could get a wide open layup and my teammates will yell at me. And my coach's name was Coach Deandre. I feel happy when my coach tells me good job too.

The End

o o o

Alisha C.
age 11

Deal With It

When I was 5 or 6 years old in kindergarten, I went to a school that was a different race as me. So on my first day everybody just kept staring at me, and when I tried to make friends, people would say, "No!" or "Why you?".
So when I went to school if I had an Afro Puff or braids, then people would just get mad at me or won't talk to me, Even the teacher! When I would ask a question about my worth, the teacher would be like figure it out yourself. So then when I came home, I asked my mom if she can straighten my hair, and she said yes.
So as soon as I got to school, then everybody started acting nice to me and the teacher just answered my questions, and everybody was just being very nice to me.
When I got home I felt weird because I kind of felt like they were Just being nice to me because I was being like them. So after that when I got to first grade at the same school, I decided to be myself and just thought they'll just have to deal with it.

Alyssa H.
age 11

Saying My Piece

Since you asked, I'll tell you why I'm so angry. I'm angry because there is so much harm and danger in the world, and I can't really do anything about it since I am just one person. All of the pollution is caused by us humans. No one is trying to fix or undo their mistakes. I want to make a difference in the world, but it's really hard because it's just going to keep occurring.

I know whoever is reading this is thinking, "Oh, this is just some silly 11-year old who doesn't know what she is talking about. The thing is— what you don't know— is that I am truly passionate about this. It is not okay that we are endangering our environment!

If we keep littering, smoking, and building, our trees will start dying. We don't want our trees to die because eventually, we won't have any more trees. Without trees, our oxygen supply will start to deplete, and our humanity rate will quickly deplete and eventually there will be no humans left on Earth.

Also, I haven't even mentioned the animals in the seas and on the Earth. There are already many sea turtles that are endangered because of us. Our city lights are affecting baby turtles after they hatch. Instead of going towards the water, they go towards roads and buildings where they quickly get run over and don't even get a chance to live their lives.

There is so much more that I have to say, but I just wanted to hit a few points in this piece. After you have read this piece, I hope you will take caution with your actions when it comes to our environment. I hope you put this piece into your thoughts.

So please, watch your thoughts because they become words.
Watch your words because they become your actions.
Watch your actions because they become your habits.
Watch your habits because they become your character.
Watch your character, because it becomes your destiny.

Amauri M.
age 9

My Cousin's House

One day I went over my cousin's house. And we was playing on his bed, and he pushed me off! I hit my back very hard on the wall, and it hurt very much!

I got very mad. And we started to fight. And that hurt too!

o o o

Amiia B.
age 13

My Hair

I am a black girl with thick, but soft 4C hair. People are so judgefull to me and hair.

First let me tell you about the struggle of having 4C hair. Gel and my hair don't like to work together. It may not look thick, but I'm telling you when she is washed and back to her natural state, can't nobody handle it but my momma because she is used to it. Oh yeah, AND I'm tender-headed, so that is just great. Take care and tender headed, thanks mom and dad for making me having to deal with this for the rest of my life.

Now let's talk about people's big mouths. People love to talk about my hair. When I have weave, people say "Ooh… is that your real hair?" Or "Girl, I feel like I've never seen your real hair before!" And when I wear my real hair, people say "Oh my God, girl! Go get your hair done!" Or, "Oh my God, why is your hair so nappy?" Knowing me Imma have to say something smart back like, "Well, at least my hair is done, lil' girl!" Or, "Boy, be quiet, because you need a line up, a new fade….actually you know what? Just get a whole new hair style."

So now you know my black girl hair struggle. What's yours?

 Saint Florian

Antonio S.
age 12

Lost in the Mall

One time I lost both my mom and my dad, in the mall.

I was looking at a squishy water ball. I looked and was attracted to the ball. I said to myself, "Hey, I am going to go look at the ball."

I walked one way, and they looked the other way, and I never noticed. I played with the ball for 5 minutes and finally noticed, turned around, and shrugged my shoulders, and kept playing for like 2 more minutes.

I was seven so even though it was my fault, I still cried and was walking around the mall. Suddenly I found a bubble gum machine, and realized I had a nickel. I put the nickel in, and it still didn't work.

I then walked around asking people for quarters. One person gave me a quarter, so I bought the bubble gum chewed it. But when the sweetness of the bubble gum went away, I started missing my parents again and started crying.

Suddenly I hear Antonio, and then I looked back, and it was my first-grade teacher Ms. Stevenson. And she bought me the squishy ball and returned me to my parents.

They apologized for the problem and made me give the ball to a kid in the foot locker place. His parents said thank you, and I walked away and started crying again.

Finally kids, just know this— don't leave your parents and get lost.

○ ○ ○

Aniyah L.
age 12

Fire Ball

The time I felt like a big ole' fire ball was in the 6th grade in 2019. Me and my group of friends almost got into a lot of fights at school 27 with the 7th graders.

OK, now before this drama happened, me and 2 girls in 7th grade was friends years back like all the way back to like when I was in 2nd or 3rd grade. Their names were Mya and Felisha (not their real names), but ANYWAY back to 2019.

So, me and my group of friends had known each other since since 1st grade, most of them like Fatima, Johnece, Tamia, known me for 6 years and my 2 besties and friend, Sajdah and Yaniyah had known me a long too.

How this all started is a new girl, Tamiah bumped into my friend and rolled her eyes. She went up to two other 7th graders and started talking about our group. We ignored it, but it kept going on, and we got irritated. We started talking about them, and how they were talking about us, and how we didn't like that.

My other friends that knew me longer than my two best friends and used to be friends with her and talked about us to them. And then she starts saying we was talking about them, and we started arguing. It didn't last that long, and they stopped being friends with her. She went to those two 7th graders and started talking about the whole group.

That's when the fireball started to grow. We started wanting to fight the 7th graders, and they wanted to fight us. Internet beef started in Group Chats, and they kept staring at us and started talking. At that point, we knew they were talking about us. And every time they sat in front of us, we knew they were talking about us.

Starting that day, we blanked out and ignored them. One day when we hear them talking about us, we got distracted and said something about them so loud so that they could hear. I told my friends to start staring and see how fast they look away. The new girl started staring at me and making a stink eye. I sometimes looked up and caught her staring and blanked out while looking at her and said "1,2,3 staring

 Saint Florian

contest!", and she rolled her eyes and looked away.

She started going out with my best friend's ex who I knew since 2nd grade. We were best friends, but then he started acting different. He started talking about me and my friends and I felt so upset and betrayed and started crying. At this point I was thinking "Why would a close friend of mine turn his back on the three closest people to him?" But, I would still help regardless.

○ ○ ○

Anyla S.
age 7

Girl Power

I'll tell you a story about a time I felt strong. I was in karate class one day and wore my white jacket and Black Belt. I was the only girl in the class, and I was a junior.

The teacher said we were going to practice kicking. He holds up a big circle, red on the outside, then, blue, then a little red circle. You're supposed to kick the little red circle. You hold your hands in front of your chest. Then you raise one foot and lean sideways. Then you kick. I kicked the red circle and I broke it. I almost kicked the teacher in the nose! My foot was right by it!

He said "Good job!" Now when we I drive by The Karate Place, I miss it because I felt strong there.

○ ○ ○

Blair A.
age 6

My Scar

I have a scar on my leg. I was running too fast. I fell. It hurt, but my friends helped me up. I bled a little bit, but I didn't cry. Instead, I was Brave. I look at the scar a lot, and when I touch it, it feels hard and kind of hurts.

○ ○ ○

Brendon M.
age 12

Tired.

The time when I had a crappy day is today. I'm tired today. I'm tired because yesterday from 7 to 10 PM, I rode a 4-wheeler. It was windy and that four wheeler is fast! I was with my cousins in a big field at a park.

After that, we ate meatloaf, corn bread, & macaroni & cheese. I slept at my cousin's house. My cousin dropped me off at camp. I had to wake up at 7:45 AM. Because I slept at my cousin's house, my bag is full of all my stuff, and I have to carry it around all day today at camp.

○ ○ ○

Brian R.
age 10

Grandma's Tacos

I feel content when I go to my grandma's house. I feel that way because on Thursdays my grandma makes me tacos. She puts cheese, meat, tomatoes, and taco sauce on my tacos. She doesn't put lettuce on them because I don't like it.

You know how when you eat tacos and the meat and cheese comes out the other side? Well, my grandma wraps it so it doesn't come out so I get to enjoy every meat, cheese, tomato, and taco sauce delicious bite!

o o o

Brielle K.
age 9

When I Busted My Lip

One random Tuesday, it was 91 degrees and it felt like 100 something. Me and my friend had a sleepover. During the sleepover, we went to a water park and made new friends and then we went to my inside pool. I went to grab a towel and "Bam!", I fell and busted my lip. I started to scream bloody murder because my lip was bleeding, and I was in huge pain. That was my story about the time I busted my lip and my bad day.

o o o

Brylen S.
age 8

The Trampoline

My favorite pair of shoes, they are white and have a Nike sign on it. And they are Air Force One's. So one time, I was outside and there was a trampoline at the park and I almost jumped in a puddle of mud. But I got closer to the trampoline, then I landed on the TRAMPOLINE, not the mud! THANK YOU!

○ ○ ○

Bryson I.
age 9

Like LeBron

So my sister she bought me Spiderman retro 1 Jordan. My mouth filled with joy. I go to school, and that was a Friday. The next day, I went to go hoop with my brother and with my brother's older friends. Only we were play to 21, and I blocked one of his friends. It felt amazing. I felt like LeBron James in my new shoes!

○ ○ ○

Bryson W.
age 9

Right Shoes, Wrong Time

My fav shoes are my pink and grey and white high tops. There my fav shoes because I don't have to tie them and I look clean in them. For some reason every time I wear them something happens.

"Dun, dun, duuun!"

One time while wearing my fav shoes, my glasses fell in slime. And another time, I fell off the monkey bars!

o O o

Caden D.
age 10

Broken Arm

I was going down the steps on my house, swinging on the handrails, and my hands slipped. I fell onto the hardwood floor, it didn't hurt, but I had a big bump on my arm. It looked weird.

I screamed; my dad came. He said, "What's wrong?"

I said, "I fell down the stairs!"

He looked at my arm. He said, "Oh my gosh!" And he put his jacket on, he put one of his over me, he got my mom and my sister, and we went to the hospital. We had to wait for the doctor. They did an x-ray, and the doctor said my arm was broke.

They put on a soft cast. They gave me medicine. I couldn't feel my arm, but when I started moving it, it hurt. I had to have the cast on like 4 or 5 weeks. I could only take it off when I got in the shower. I had to write with my left hand in school. It was terrible. For tests, the special needs teacher helped me. I couldn't play basketball, so I got to be the assistant coach.

Carson S.
age 6

King Carson

My brother punched me, and it made me feel like I was bleeding. There was pain in my body and my heart. My brother punched me in the stomach too. My mom takes away his phone.

In boxing, I punch people on the cheek because that's what boxers are supposed to do. My mom was happy that I won. I was proud, but I was still mad that my brother punched me.

I felt the venom in my body. I punched my brother in the back in boxing. After that they called me King Carson. I got a trophy.

○ ○ ○

Christian S.
age 5

Best Mom Ever

Since you ask I'll tell you why my mommy makes me happy. She buys me toys. She bought me a bed, and she puts a lot of blankets and black panther pillows on my bed. My mom is the BEST!

○ ○ ○

Christopher H.
age 6

Grandpa & Me

My grandpa was special to me, because when I went to his house, he always gave me candy and treats like Sour Patch Kids and chocolate. He always told me that when he dies, he will always be watching me. He always carried something handy for him to help other people. When he died, I cried half the day. I went to the funeral. Then I thought about him and felt happy. When I was 5, I asked my dad if my grandpa was still watching me. He said, "Yes and God was too."

o o o

Colton A.
age 8

Crabby Colton

One time when I was 8, I was in Florida. On the first day I was so stressed, but we walked to this place called Crabby Bill's. The French Toast tasted so gross, and the sweet tea tasted like gross air. I was so crabby after I ate. Crabby Bill's made me crabby!

Then we went to the beach, and that beach was called the Great Beach. But to me, it had to much seaweed. But me my sister and my dad went really far out, and we played this game called...Bob and we had to bob over the waves. We had a lot of fun and it was a really funny game. And it was a Great Beach!

o o o

Da'laysia G.
age 11

If I Was in Charge

Since you ask, I tell you why I am angry.

At summer camp, we have roles like the Mayor, Deputy Mayor, and Budget Director. They pick the people they think are strict. When one of them gets picked, it is the same person from last year. If they tell someone to be quiet, they end up talking. But if they told someone else to be quiet, Gosh!

When they chose the people for the roles, they picked the same people from last year. I was like "Oh my gosh. Same people, and I am not talking about only a couple! Same exact people!"

Anyways, when they picked the same people I thought to myself "another angry summer at summer camp." The reason this makes me so angry is because it is like they forget about the rest of the people who have not yet got to be a Mayor or Budget Director and Deputy Mayor.

If I was in charge of picking the people I would pick new people who don't take advantage of their job, and I would pick them by the way the act. When choosing the Mayor, I want someone that... does not take advantage, is fun, but when it is time to get down to business, then they get down to business.

Danae'sha R.
age 8

Muddy Shoes

One day me and my baby cousin went to the playground, and I went to the swings. It was muddy on the swings. But, I took a risk, and I jumped in the muddy, and my shoes was all muddy, and my mom was mad. And my shoes almost fell off!

○ ○ ○

Darien W.
age 11

Wake Up!

There is a silver light in my room that wakes me up. My mom walks in the room and touches it, and the room lights up. My eyes stay closed. So my mom walks up to my bed and shakes my leg. Then I wake up and see the light in my eyes. I pull the covers back up and try to go back to sleep, but my mom takes off the cover and drags me up. She says "Get up," so I get up and go to the bathroom. I take a shower, but it doesn't wake me up. I go eat breakfast, but it doesn't wake me up either. My mom drives me to summer camp. I try to sleep on the way, but I wake up every time she steps on the brake. We get to summer camp early. I'm still tired. I might wake up when I get to the pool.

○ ○ ○

 Saint Florian

Darion S.
age 10

Just My Luck

I am going to write about when I got a scar on my knee. First, let me tell you how I got it. I was outside playing basketball, and then the ball was about to go into the street so I hurried up—but, I tripped over a rock.

My leg had a little slant in it, and there was blood every on the sidewalk. I was only 4 years old. Next, they rush me to the hospital. I was lucky because my mom is a doctor and nurse and my grandma to0, and they stitched my leg with 5 stitches. But I ain't gonna lie— that stuff hurt me so bad that I cried the whole time.

Then, I felt better a few days later. Now, I don't have the scar anymore.

Edosa E.
age 12

Saint Florian

Since you ask, I'll tell you why I'm so excited. Because I can be here at the Saint Florian camp. It'sso fun! You can talk, eat, meet new kids, go on field trips.

I met two kids named Isiah and Brandon. Isiah has a little sister named Zwi and a little brother named Isaac— they are good kids. We talk to each other, we laugh, we play. It's so exciting to be here at this camp. I said I didn't want to be here, but it has changed my life.

I met a lot of kids here. Some of them I talk too, and some of them I don't and that's fine. I'm glad that my summer is going great. I don't have to be here on the weekends, but I talk to kids on my phone and I watch TV and other things.

Some things that I don't like here, but I still get through it. It's not that fun sometimes here, and I don't like it. On the first day here, I was nervous because I didn't know anybody. I think everybody was new here. It was cool on the first day, because I met one person, then I got through the day. I went here again, and it got better and better than on the first day.

Today I think is going to be good. I think some days it is always good, and some other days it is not good for me. I'm still new, and I got other things to learn.

The last part is the Saint Florian is a good camp for kids to learn things about other kids. What I like the most about the camp is spending time talking to other kids about good things. The specific thing about this camp is to learn and have a great time, and I think everybody likes this camp the end.

○ ○ ○

Emery W.
age 7

Skating with Grandma

I was in Tennessee, and I was skating. Then I won the race, and I got a free drink. My grandma raced too. She did not win, but we had a good time. The end.

○ ○ ○

Counselor Erica W.

The First Time I Started At Saint Florian Camp

I saw different shirt colors and many counselors, who were kind and nice. I really thought to myself "Nice order, kind of loud, and how in the world will this camp teach such structure?"

So when Firefighter Tony asked me to drive for the camp, I said "Yes" not knowing this was a leadership camp. I learned the motto, the philosophy, the creed, and the ten leadership principles. I asked myself:

"Are you a leader?"
"What are your intentions?"
"What was your purpose to become a leader and build up my own character?"

The Writer's Center came, and I said to myself, "What?"
But, I started my writing in June 2009. Today is July 10, 2019. This is my second paper I have written. Enjoy Mrs. Lyn Jones!

From Miss Lyn to Counselor Erica: I enjoyed this very much. Thank you for sharing your story and words with us. And I'm so grateful for your leadership and service. You were meant to lead!

Ethan M.
age 8

Best Friend Ever

At my best day ever, I learned how to skate and made my best friend ever. The first day at camp, I was nervous, I didn't know what to do. I didn't know what to say. So I just sat in my chair, but a couple hours later, I got the hang of the camp. I made a friend, and I played with him a lot. I talked to him on the bus and in the cafeteria a lot.

o o o

Graham "Otis" A.
age 6

My Brother

I love my mom and my dad. I love my brother, because we play basketball together. But I'm mad, because he dunked and bent the rim all the way to the pole. My brother taught me how to play basketball. He is fourteen. He compliments me and makes me feel good. My brother inspired me to play basketball.

o o o

Graham A.
age 9

Baby Jett

It was March 30, and my dad was rushed to the hospital. And he rushed quickly to the hospital. Then he got there, and he said "We're here, honey!"

Then they went and they had to stay for a long time that day. Me my sister and my little brother were playing in the house then our Nana came in the house and said, "We got pizza!" We ate the pizza very fast, then we watch Little Dias. It was so sad then we went to sleep.

When I woke up, we got some donuts. Then they called us and said "Hi kids. we are coming home in 2 hours." Then we got lunch, and our lunch was so good. Then someone knocked on the door, and it was our new baby brother. I was so happy. And his name is Jett.

○ ○ ○

Isaac J.
age 7

Grandma

My grandma has black hair. Her skin is like peaches. She sometimes she uses glasses when she's reading. Sometimes she reads to me. It my favorite book about a mouse that goes to find a big apple. The book makes me feel happy. I sit on my grandma's lap. Me and my brother and sister like to play with her. We play somersaults. My grandma does somersaults too. She does funny things. Sometimes she says I'm being good. And that makes me feel happy.

Isaiah J.
age 10

SNAP!

So it was the middle of kindergarten, and my day wasn't going so well. I had applesauce, AND I hate applesauce. I thought it was going to get better at recces. Until... I was playing angry bird I.R.L. with my friends Elijah and Clayton. I ran into the crimson red foam wall... and... SNAP! My pinky was sprained. It felt like my pinky was jammed! And smashed by a hammer! An hour later I had to leave with my mom, but it still hurt so bad! I couldn't move or feel my pinky. When we got to the hospital I had my Lunchable. After about 5 minutes they called me up... they used an X-ray and talked to me. That's when I heard I sprained my pinky. I still went to school and it was fine in about a few weeks.

o o o

Isaiah B.
age 13

Dear Future Self

Dear Isaiah,

Ten years from now, you should be a starter for the Los Angeles Lakers as a point guard or a shooting guard, making at least 141 million dollars.

After that, I will buy my dad his dream car, a Bugatti Super Sport. Me and him will have the same car, then I will buy my dad and his wife a house in the Los Angeles Hills.

And me?

I will have a mansion in a suburban complex. I will have three kids, and I will be married. I will have a really big pool with a basketball court with an indoor movie theater with a guest house for the visitors, and I will have a really big trampoline.

Israel C.
age 6

Sleepy

Since you asked, I'll tell you about when I was so sleepy. When I woke up, I was sleepy. When I'm sleepy, I can't even stand up. I can't even eat! I can't even open or close my eyelids. I go to bed every night at 9:00 p.m., but wake up at different times. I like to go to sleep. I like to go to sleep every day. When I am sleepy, my whole body hurts, especially my feet.

○ ○ ○

Ja'Lan K.
age 13

Feeling Better

I was in the 7th grade and was on the 7th grade football team. The school that I went to was called Stoneybrook Middle School. I was making decent enough grades to stay on the football team, but they still wasn't good enough for me to feel good about them.

When football season ended, my grades dropped lower than what they were. When I would be in school, I would be feeling like I'm doing good; but all of my test and quiz scores would still be lower than average. I would stay up late at night to finish my homework and to study for classes.

I started to give up, because I felt like I would never pass. After the first semester, I moved to a different school. The school was called Creston Middle School. When I switch grades, I started to improve more and more. In the middle of school, I started to make better grades, and I stopped feeling like I would never pass. Eventually I started to make the A and B honor roll. I started to feel good about myself again. Me my mom and grandparents started feeling proud about myself.

Jada K.
age 6

Florida

It was my first time at Florida. I was sitting on the thingy, and I was swinging on it. And I fell backward, and I hit my head, my back, and my shoulder.

At the beach, first, everybody put down their towel and then they took off their flip-flops. So, I run to the ocean and then some people got salt water in their mouth. I feel nasty because the salt water came out of my mouth. I was jumping when the waves was coming. I wasn't jumping really high. And I got buried in sand. My cousins Josiah and Jathen buried me.

o o o

James G.
age 9

Unstoppable

A time I felt tough was when I was in the YMCA basketball. I was in practice and my coach said I was doing good.

I keep trying, and I shot a 3 pointer and made it.

I felt tough with my basketball skills. And I felt unstoppable for a whole week. I also feel tough when I practice at home. Every time I practice, I say I need to be better than my dad. My dad shoots like trash, but I shoot like "wet water" swish.

Jarin P.
age 6

My New Shoes

I was at the mall with my dad. We went into the store, and he bought me some blue Jordans. I said, "I love you." And he said "I love you, too." I put them on. They feel like they have a fluffy Tiger in them to make me run fast like a Cheetah.

Later we went to a party and I wore my new shoes. People said, "They look good." That made me feel good. When I'm 26, I will have my own treehouse and I'll be living in the wild and have Tigers and Cheetahs.

○ ○ ○

Jason S.
age 11

Since You Asked

The first time I went outta town was when I went to Mississippi for my sister's college interview. When we went it was a 7 to 8 hour drive. I was asleep for most of the time, so it was quick. But what was not quick was my sister not shutting up! She kept talking about it. it took her about 4 hours to close her mouth. When we got there, we stayed in a hotel and there was a pool. I begged and begged to go, but never went that day. That night, we went to Applebee's, I think. After that, I slept on the chair— but I got to watch TV so it was fun.

The next day we woke up and went to breakfast that was in the hotel— it was good. After that we went to the college and walked around. That took a long time, and my legs started to hurt. But after that I finally got to go to the pool. We were swimming for a really long time, and my legs started to hurt more.

Then we were on our way home, so we went to Mcdonald's to go get food. I bet you thought the day was over, but NO, my sister wanted to go to the mall. But the day was over, and we got home around 8 o'clock.

Jathen T.
age 10

Hammocks in Atlanta

Since you asked I'll tell you when I've felt calm. I went to Atlanta, Georgia. I went there to see my cousin. He is older than my grandma—don't know how. He's like 70 something and my grandma is 61; that's crazy!

Well, that's not what this story is really about. I was helping him put the hammock up in the middle of two trees… but you already know what did. I laid down on it at "yup that's exactly what I did." A few minutes flyed by, but It felt like seconds. What's going on?

So, let me explain what's going on. I'm in Atlanta, Georgia at my cousin's house in his awesome customized backyard on his green hammock. And I'm just rocking, and soon as I know, it I hear a bird chirping "chirp, chirp," and I'm like "Okay, well I just gonna go to sleep". And that's what I did. I woke and I seen my cousin's cat in my face, so I got up went inside the house and watched a movie, the Secret Life of Pets.

THE END.

○ ○ ○

Jayden J.
age 10

First Day

Since you asked, I'll tell you why I'm so nervous. I'm so nervous, because it's my first day here, and I don't know what to do. Like when I got here, I was confused, and I didn't know where to sit or what to say. I feel like a turtle in a shell, too scared to come out. I am being very quiet, because I talk to myself even though there are two people by me. I

I wonder when I will push through, because it feels like an eternity. Last night I was so pumped to come to camp. But, I didn't know what it will be like; now it's nothing like I imagined. I feel like I need friends, but I don't know anybody's name. I feel like it's going to take forever to get out of this slump.

○ ○ ○

Jeffrey A.
age 10

Orlando

One day when my grandpaw said we were going to Orlando, Florida, I thought that we were going for a day or two, so I wasn't very excited. But then he said we were staying for two weeks, and then we went on the plane. And the last plane was the best, so we were happy because they had tablets and headphones to give us so we could hear.

And when we got there it wasn't too hot for me, because we didn't really do anything on the first day. When we got there, it was 102 degrees, and as soon as we went to the pool we all jumped in, and then we got out we went in the Hilton Apartment. They were already making dinner, and after the good meal, my sister went to pick up a snake, and then before we came we saw a chameleon climbing up the tree. And the best part was we went to Disney World for all the rest of the days.

Jeremiah K.
age 11

Mad & Glad

Since you asked, I'll tell you why I'm so mad.

I had my game taken away for because I bought V-bucks. I was on punishment, but I did all out on my chores, dishes and stuff.

Since you asked me, I'll tell you why I'm happy!

I got my game back. When I don't have my game, I feel like life is boring.

o o o

Jeremiah O.
age 6

Bravery

The time I was brave was when a bully hit me. I had told my mom, and she said, "We'll have to talk to his mom." His mom said, "Go to your room for punishment." And it made me happy, because he couldn't be mean to me anymore.

o o o

Jermaine W.

age 8

Losing Grandma

I lost my grandma when I was about five, and that was dreadful because I never got to see her again. But when I go to heaven, I can see her. My cousin Jay told me, and I was so sad but now I feel comfy when I talk about it. When I lost my grandma, it was dreadful until the last few minutes because I realized she was in heaven, and it was ok, and I will see her one day. At the funeral, everyone was crying, so I started crying. When I saw her there, I missed her. I still wish I had my grandma.

o o o

Jordan T.

age 8

Paper Planes

I was bored and had papers, so I kept on folding them. I folded them a bunch, and it looked like a stick. But I unfolded it a bit, and it looked like a paper airplane. I was super happy when I saw it was an airplane, and that's why I keep doing it. I just have a lot of fun making paper airplanes. I was one years old when I started folding paper airplanes. I even made a thousand of them!

o o o

Joseph A.
age 11

Need I Say More?

Since you asked, I'll tell you why I'm tired. It's Monday morning, need I say more? Me trying to get up on a Monday is like trying to peel glued duck tape off a wall. I tend to be a bit moody on Mondays— I mean who isn't?

○ ○ ○

Josiah T.
age 6

My Cousin's Shoes

I felt happy because my cousin said I could have his shoes. He couldn't fit in them, and I could. They're white and they have four Velcro straps. They're basketball shoes ,and I run really fast in them. I wash them off with a baby wipe every day. And I love them.

○ ○ ○

Juliana M.
age 8

Gammie's House

When I was watching TV one day, my mom said you're going to Gammie's house. So I said, "Yay!" So when it was tomorrow, I put on my clothes, brushed my teeth, and put on deodorant. So when we got there, I see my cousin Jada so me and my cousin went to get some Slushies. We both picked all of the three flavors. But when we got them, they was brown but still good. So when we was in the car, we was playing. We got dolls at Gammie's house, and when it was night time we played with our dolls and fell asleep.

 Saint Florian

Kaiden S.
age 18

Missing Sega

This is a story about when I lost my favorite game. I lost my favorite game two years ago. I had this game called Sega, my favorite game on Sega is Michael Jackson Moon Walker. It didn't need Wi-Fi, the game was very old. My mom had it when she was 6 years old. I went upstairs in the guest room, and I played it in there. Then two days later, it was missing. I looked in my mom's room, my sister's room. Then my sister found it. I was so happy! Then my mom bought me a case for it.

○ ○ ○

Kailey P.
age 11

The No Fright Friday Night

What I'm going to tell you about is a time when I felt content without no worries. It was Friday, March 8, 2019 (One day after something exciting happened), and I remember it like it was yesterday. That day was the Students versus the Teachers basketball game at JTV Hill.

When I got there, the game had already started (which really sucked). When I walked in, one of my best friends (her name is Sara) said, "Hey!" and showed me where the rest of my friends were sitting. It was just me, and my friends Sara, Malachi, Zien, Maddie, and my "brother", Andrew.

When I sat down, I sat right by Sara and Andrew. (Now really quick I'm going to let you guys in on a secret, Sara and Andrew were "together"). Sara then tapped on my shoulder and said "I want to hold Andrew's hand, but I don't know how". So I started talking to Andrew, and he was down with it, but when I moved from between Sara and Andrew, it was time for Sara to go home. DUN DUN DUNNNN!!!

Andrew was so sad, but I could NOT stop laughing!!! Then a little later me and Andrew were talking about my "crush" (let's call him Henry). The next thing I know, it's time for me to go and guess who walks through the door…Henry!!! Then when Andrew saw him he said "Kailey ouuouu!!! I said, "OMG SHUT UPPP," while laughing.

So when my mom came over (cuz I was taking soooo long apparently), I begged to stay for at least five more minutes, and she let me, but we ended up staying THE WHOLE GAME. (Which was AMAZING!). When Henry sat down, he sat next to me, and Andrew started playing the song from the Lion King that goes "Can you feel the love tonight…"

When that was over (because he played the WHOLE SONG), I had told Andrew, "I want to hold Henry's hand." But didn't know if Henry wanted to hold my hand. So when I told Andrew he said, "I got you lil sis." (because we call each other family). So we switched seats, so that Andrew was sitting between me and Henry. It seemed like Andrew was talking to Henry for the longest time (or I was just really nervous).

Soon me and Andrew switch seats and he said "Kailey, put your hand on the bleachers" (that's where we were sitting) I had asked "Why"; And Andrew said "You'll see". So I just started to watch the basketball game (Yes it was still going on, it was 3rd Quarter and the 8th GRADE STUDENTS WERE LOSING BAD). The next thing I know I feel a hand pick up mine. I look at my hand and guess who was holding my hand?! I looked over to Andrew and whispered "thx," and he replied with "no problem lil sis." When I looked over to Henry I see him, not only smiling but BLUSHING. It felt like I was in heaven!

When the game ended, (btw the teachers won, I know right hard to believe since they are like 1,000 years old), a couple of my friends and Henry and I played some basketball and it was 3v3: Me, Henry and Andrew, against Malachi, Zien, and Keegan. Keegan said that he would guard me because he thinks that I suck.

When we were checking up, all I did was a simple cross-over and he fell. I could NOT stop laughing, and neither could anybody else. After the 3v3 game, it was time for Henry to go. He walked up to me gave me a hug goodbye and said "I'll text you later." I said "ok", and just smiled. When I turned around I looked at Andrew, and he started singing "Kailey; could you feel the love tonight", and I said "OMG SHUT UP," while laughing.

Honestly that night was one of the BEST NIGHTS OF MY WHOLE LIFE

Landon H.
age 9

When I Was Scared

Since you asked, I'll tell you about a time when I was scared.

When I was in boy scouts, I was scared of sleeping. But when I went to camp. I wasn't scared.

O O O

Layla W.
age 8

Happy Birthday

A time when I was really happy and content was on my 5th birthday. It was a unicorn party. My cousins and parents were there. We played hide and go seek. We got to eat pepperoni pizza, my favorite kind of pizza. I got a pink hoverboard and an iPad. I got a unicorn cover too! My favorite part was when everyone sang Happy Birthday to me! I also got a unicorn swimsuit. They also surprised me with a unicorn slide. I really like unicorns, because they're colorful. I also had a unicorn cake with a purple horn, it tasted like vanilla. It was fun.

O O O

LeiLani R.
age 7

Sister Love

When I am sad, my sisters help me. I play with my sister when I am sad. When I was sad, my sister makes me happy. When I am with my sister, I feel good. My soul is happy my heart beats fast because I am loved. They make me feel good. I know they love me by their love. Skating and the jumping gym are our favorite places to go. At the pool, I do cannonballs and my sister does sometimes. My sisters help me when I'm nervous. Sister love.

Lexi A.
age 10

Girl Fight

In our class, there was a bully. I won't say her name, but she picked on everybody. Especially another girl; I won't say that name either. I was assigned to be with the two girls to play the game Spot-it. Then a fight started to happen. I hate girl fights! It started out when the bully said something. Out of nowhere she said "You're not the boss of me."

"I wasn't even bossing you," said the other girl angrily.

"Well you do," said the bully.

This seemed to go on forever, when finally I said… "Stop doing that to her; she's one of my best friends."

Then she said, "Make me." I said, "Oh I will, I'll go tell the teacher".

She said, "I'll hurt you." I said "Ok" and went to tell the teacher. Then the teacher came out and punished the bully. The point is, I stood up for my friend, she was happy and we played alone, away from the bully.

Madison S.
age 6

Sunday with Dad

On Sunday, I got to see my dad. It was so fun because we got to see Toy Story 4. I wish I could see my dad every day. I went again. And we went to the park, and I went on the swing and after I got off the swing, my dad take me and my sister and brother to the pool. I can only swim in three feet, but it is so fun. Then he took us to McDonald's. I got a Happy Meal, and I got chicken nuggets and fries.

o o o

Makail M.
age 12

Confidence

I always had a lot of confidence in the way I looked, walked, talked, and even the way I acted. But what really what makes me feel good is when someone tells me I am smart. Plenty of people have told me that since I was like way younger than I am now, but they still do in 2019.

I don't really know why I feel so good in myself when someone ever tells me that. But I honestly think it is because I work for the grades I earned. I want like A's and maybe B's. But I also think that when people call me that—smart—then I feel like that I am very powerful and I can do whatever I want with being smart and having good grades.

I really do feel proud of myself when being called smart. The feeling of being proud of myself from when people call me smart is like the feeling of someone giving you a dog or something you really wanted for Christmas or your birthday or something like that. I love being called smart because not many people may be called that. But everyone is capable of being called that. If either because they don't try, or because they do try but just not at that point yet.

I feel like if everyone was to be called smart, like I do then everyone may have the same feeling as I do or it just might be me that has that feeling and everyone else doesn't really care if they got a compliment, or they're just not really used to being called the word "smart" by people.

But I think everyone should appreciate being called smart because it may just be a once in a lifetime feeling. So you should take it as if it was the last time. But like I said I am also confident in the way I look.

By My Side

I hope I will never leave my mom and dad. I love my mom and dad so much, and if I would lose either of them, I would feel heartbroken and cry so much like never before.

My heart would sink all the way down my stomach and to my leg and then to my foot and out my body. And my heart would never come back to the spot it is supposed to be at.

I would hate to leave my mom and dad. I love them so so so so so much, and I feel that I could never lose them as long as I'm living. My parents have always been by my side since I came from the hospital. And without them, I wouldn't even be here writing on this piece of paper.

So I am so grateful for my mom and dad. I do worry about my dad a lot because he is in the Army and goes to war sometimes, and that really worries me because I can lose someone very important to me who brought me to this Earth that I am on right now.

But as long as I stay positive, then I know he will still be on my side no matter what. There are a lot of reasons I love my parents like because they are loving, caring, helpful, just amazing, awesome, and so much more.

But most importantly is that they are the best parents in the world no matter what anyone else says. Because I know they are the best parents in the world, and I never ever want to lose them in my whole life. And I know they feel the same way about me.

o o o

Marcel M.
age 7

Resee Cup

My dog, Tyson, had no friends until my dad bought this dog named Reese Cup. She was shy. She was shy for 5 whole days. Now Reese Cup and my other dog both play together. They have food bowls and drink bowls. Reese always drinks from Tyson's bowl. She tries to eat my food and my sister's. Once she jumped on the table and got my sister's Lunchable! My sister said "No, Reese!" Reese still stared at my sister and wanted more. Then my mommy put her in the cage. Reese wanted to come out the cage and kept staring at anyone who passed until they let her out.

She started playing with Tyson again, and then I fed them their food and drink. Then they got to play, and they started to chase my sister. My sister kept screaming. Somebody came at the door. They was both barking. It was my cousin. My cousin got scared, and then they put them both in the cage. They had to stay in the cage the rest of the day.

○ ○ ○

Maya B.
age 10

Cousin Dorothy

My cousin Dorothy had cancer. She was a nurse when women didn't have rights. My grandpa (G-Mac) had cancer too. He beat it and got it again. My G-Mac turned 70 in November. I saw my cousin Dorothy there, and I was happy. Two months later, cousin Dorothy died of cancer, and I didn't even know she had it. Now every day, I go over to my G-Mac's house. There is a picture of Dorothy on the stand. In the Bible, Jesus helped a really ill girl heal so, since G-Mac didn't have cancer two weeks later, I think that my cousin Dorothy helped my G-Mac.

Mianna S.
age 11

My Scar

So I was visiting my grandpa in Florida, and I fell asleep on the plane and when I got out my grandpa was waiting at the airport. I gave him a great big hug. Once we pulled in the driveway, I got out the car and ran straight inside and hugged the puppies.

Then when I got situated. I ran straight out the backyard and went to my tree house. I was trying to climb up and slipped on a step and fell straight in a bush of thorns. I was crying so loud and calling my mom's name.

Once she ran outside, she grabbed me and called my grandpa and rushed me to the hospital and the doctor has to cut my leg open cause there were a lot of thorns in it. Then they cleaned it and stitched it. Then I got a cast and had to learn how to walk on that leg so that's my scar story.

o o o

Pharaoh P.
age 6

Lamborghini

One day I was out at my Grandma's house, and I fell down the stairs. I couldn't stop myself, and I almost ran into some plants that my grandma really likes. I was trying to scoot down the stairs in a dangerous way. I was at the top of the stairs and I tried to slide down with my eyes closed.

At the bottom of the stairs, I got slower but I still landed in the basement. So I called my grandma, and she ran to me and caught me. I told my Grandma I was scared because I felt like I was going fast like a Lamborghini or any fast car. The stairs were pushing on my body and it felt terrible. But I was okay like two minutes later.

Pheldon M.
age 6

Hot Wheels Birthday

I was really happy and content during my 4th birthday. It was a Hot Wheels party. Everyone surprised me! I got an Xbox and it had Roblox, but the first thing I played was vehicle simulator. My parents, Godbrother Stephen, and Uncle Marcus were there. Pretty much everyone in my family was there. I was horrified by all the people singing "Happy Birthday," but it was fun. I even had a Thomas and Friends cake, and it was chocolate.

○ ○ ○

Preslie-Jai A.
age 12

Where's Preslie!?

There was a time my auntie and I were at Disneyland for a family vacation. It was a surprise. We also stayed at the hotel. We walked down to the elevator and we were off on our way to Disney.

I jumped on my Auntie's back and put sunscreen on. We started to walk in to the entrance. Then my Auntie stopped. I was wondering, why but I didn't say nothing.

Then she started screaming. "PRESLIE" "WHERE IS PRESLIE." She was spinning around like crazy, and I thought I was going to vomit.

Everyone was looking at us crazy, and they were all laughing too. But then I said "I'm right here, Auntie!"

Everyone in my family started to laugh. Ever since that day, we always bring it up when she's around.

Quanell C.
age 11

My Bad Day

The time when I had a bad day was when it was the fall. It was cold that day. My Nana did not like all the hair on my head, so she made me cut all of it off.

I had no hat, so my head was cold. I was mad! It took almost three years to grow my hair back.

Not all my hair is back yet. For those three years my head was cold. I like long hair because it keeps my head warm.

o o o

Raven R.
age 11

Dolley

One time when I felt peaceful was when I got my new cat. She was a mix of all types. She knew when you were sad, and she would comfort you by licking your toes. It felt like sandpaper was wet and was scraping your toes. She would also come to you if you were on the floor playing video games. Or watching TV. She would also would smooch off your water if it was on the floor.

o o o

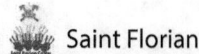 Saint Florian

Saniia F.

age 8

Suprise!

Since you ask, I'll tell you why I am so excited! When my family surprised me with a unicorn birthday party, I was very surprised. There were five people there, and they said "Happy Birthday!". Then, we had some cake.

The unicorn cake was awesome! And they also had brownies to surprise me. Secret… it was a home-made cake. My favorite part was when they told me to go upstairs and watch TV and then they told me "close your eyes and come downstairs." and I went to the kitchen and opened my eyes and saw everything!

Next, we drove around the city.

o o o

Sevan W.

age 11

Mr. Willy Wayne's Holy Fried Chicken

The only reason that I go to church on special days is that my mom makes me, and we get Mr. Willie Wynne's Holy Fried Chicken. His Fried Chicken makes me see Jesus when I close my eyes. It's like a heavenly angel threw some golden chicken on my tongue.

Whenever he would be cooking and we'd be having service and we'd hear gospel music, we all knew it was Mr. Willie Wynne, and I guess that the gospel music seeped into the chicken because that chicken was fire.

Skylar B.
age 13

Timeline Ending

Since you asked, I'll tell you why I'm so fed up. I'm fed up because by the time I'm out of high school, everything will be messed up. As Bill Nye said, the world is on fricking fire. People make laws that are stupid and no one can get along.

Oh yeah, I'm not really joking about the Earth basically melting. In 21 years, most of the ice caps will melt, and the water will completely cover Florida. Do you know how sad we'll be without Florida? We won't have any stories of stupid people doing stupid things or Disney World.

People are making stupid laws and hurting people for no reason. Alabama made the abortion [law], which frankly, I somewhat expected, but it's scary because then other states might do the same thing. It's like a Domino Effect, except with overpopulation and foster care.

The one thing that ticks me off the most is how NO ONE can get along. There is one drama after drama, controversy after controversy, and I get so burnt out from all the tea that I just didn't go on YouTube for a week.

Like really. It was that bad.

I just wanna watch wholesome videos but no, YouTube just HAD to pop off constantly.

This is why I'm so fed up!

Finger Long Gone

I was a dumb kid. Like extremely stupid. I cried once because I locked myself in the bathroom. You'd think "A kid can't get dumber than that, right?" Well, you are absolutely, positively, without a doubt, wrong. So let me tell you about how I cut off my finger!

I was about five or six when this happened. And out of all the places it could've happened, it happened in a church. It was after services, and we went upstairs to cut cardboard paper eggs. I think this was before Easter, so it makes sense about the egg cutting.

All the kids went into a green room with old wooden tablets all around. I sat down in a chair and waited for the Pastor's wife to hand out scissors to all of us. When she got to me, she told me "Oh, we don't have any safety scissors, you can just use the adult scissors."

Of course, being a big dumb kid and wanting to be a grown up, I said "OK!" and took the child meat cleavers.

The finger holes were firetruck red, and the blade was the size of my baby hands side-by-side. I then put my hands in the giant hand holders and started cutting the dark green paper in front of me.

Well, I only got five chops in before I gave a big chop to my middle finger. I pulled my hand back, with no expression whatsoever, and looked at the nub that was gushing blood like expensive fireworks.

Luckily, my mom came in the room and dragged me to the ER.

The last thing that I remember is walking out of a hospital room with a pretty holographic band-aid on my finger. To this day, my middle finger is still crooked.

I think that's the reason why I don't go to that church anymore. :')

o o o

Sonnie T.
age 11

My Mother

The one time someone said something good to me— to make me feel good about myself— is my mother. My mom always encourages me to be the best that I can. She is always positive in negative situations. She is like the smiley face in the dark section.

So, let me get deeper. When I found out that my parents were separating, I felt broken. It felt like half of me just split open. I was hurt. I had the biggest attitude ever. I didn't listen to a thing anybody said to me. I've been used to my parents married for so long that I got stuck.

Until my mother pulled me to the side and hugged me. She said "It's going to be okay." I calmed down wiped my tears and hugged her back. When we were done she asked me, "Am I okay?"

I sniffled and said "Yes." My mother is the best mother ever. Even when I am very, very, very mad at something, I still love her. And that is the one person who makes me feel good.

○ ○ ○

Taryn J.
age 10

Granddad

A few months ago, my Granddad was in the hospital because my Grandma said that my Granddad hit his head so hard that he had to go to the hospital.

I got sad when my mom told me and my sister. We didn't get to see him because he lives in St. Louis. If I could go see him, I could make him feel better and feel loved. I would hug him.

I was in a puddle of tears when I found out, but I knew when things was better and he wasn't feeling no more pain.

Taylor J.
age 7

Pranked!

The time my sister pranked me is a good story. She had it made so when I walked in, a bucket of flour, it poured on my head. I had to take a shower to get it off, But, I got her back with a water balloon!

○ ○ ○

Tazae H.
age 7

Camp Takeover

This is a story about a time I felt totally happy. We took over at camp (Saint Florian). We stayed on the conduct clock for five days. We had to take a test, and if everybody got it right, we got to take over. We did it!

We went to Great Times. We went golfing, played some of the games, and I played a fighting game. At the end of camp, we went to a cabin and on the last week of camp, the whole camp got a $23,000 check of donations. That made me so happy!

Oh, and we got a pizza party! Then we got ice cream AND the white bus. It made me happy because we were working hard and it all paid off. We went to Cincinnati in the new bus.

On the last day we had had activities that were fun.

○ ○ ○

Troy W.
age 12

Feeling Brave

I went to King's Island. It was my first time. I saw these cool rollercoasters. I went to the kiddy place, and I saw a fast, fast rollercoaster.

I felt brave because I've been on a big rollercoaster at the fair. I went to the scary car place where all the monsters are. Then I went on the car, and I saw all these creepy monsters so I hid inside the car. By the time that I popped up, it was all over. When I left, I felt kinda scared.

Then I went back to it I thought, I would go every time. But I saw this other rollercoaster that went really fast. It had a kitty's face on it. Then I went on it, and it went loopity-loop and around. I was feeling brave because it was so cool.

Then I went on the big, big rollercoaster. I felt brave because I went on the kid ones so I felt ready for the big one.

○ ○ ○

Uriah T.
age 9

Swimming

I like swimming at the pool because I like how I can move in the water. It's like I'm on the moon. I can do hand stands under the water and front flips. Swimming is also my favorite thing to do. I can't always go swimming so I also like to play pool with my Dad and my brother. And the last time I went swimming was last Wednesday. I forgot what I was wearing but I was on a field trip at camp because we did good. I did a lot of hand stands, and we all took swimming lessons to see if we needed a floaty. And, I did not need a floaty so I swam without one. I also think everyone had a good time after JC's went, the Core went and then tomorrow the Cash gets to go swimming too.

 Saint Florian

Weston F.
age 9

Great Wolf Lodge

Excited!!! Because my family will go to Great Wolf Lodge ,and it is going to be fun, and I'm going to have fun on the waterslides, and I going to have fun at the pool, and we'll sleep in a cabin, and the cabins have bunkbeds, and me and my brother and me are going to play in the water, and I've never been there.

○ ○ ○

Xavier
age 9

Baseball Cards

Since you asked, I'll tell you why I'm so happy. One day at the store I told my dad, "Can you buy me six-hundred basketball cards?" I already had 500, already spent $10,000 dollars on basketball cards. I begged my dad and mom for ten months in a row. My dad said, "I am getting tired of your asking me." So I got them. I went to my friend's house, and I sorted are basketball cards and I had more!

○ ○ ○

Zaiya M.
age 12

Butterfly Necklace

I love my dad, and I know he loves me too. But when I was six, my parents split. It was two years later when I'd actually got to see him again. It was my ninth birthday party, and I knew he was coming. I'd heard that he'd become a sales person and made a decent amount of moneu. I thought that it was probably going to be a toy, since he had to also buy a present for my cousin because we were sharing a birthday.

But I was wrong. When we first entered Great Times, he was standing there with a small box. Inside was a gold necklace with a butterfly charm. I didn't have any jewelry so this started my collection.

But here's the sad part; I also lost it. It was a blazing hot day, and I was ready to get off the bus when my hand accidently sliced the chain in half. I didn't notice at first, but while inside my house, my necklace fell to the floor. I stared at it for a while, then started crying very silently.

After about three minutes, I quickly wiped my tears, picked up the necklace and detached the charm from the chain. I put it in my jewelry box and a few days later, it was gone. I was so upset that I confessed that I lost and broke it to my mother and father. About two weeks ago I found the chain but the charm was long gone.

o o o

Zarriah M.
age 11

Joselyn

Everyone has a best friend or a friend that is really close. My best friend is Joselyn. We both enjoy similar things and activities. When you have a best friend, you have a lot of good memories, but with the good memories also comes the bad.

It was the end of May, I was on my phone playing a game with Joselyn, and that's when the bad memory happened. Somehow, we got into an argument and it got so bad that she said she couldn't be friends with me. As soon as I saw those words on the screen of my phone, my heart dropped to the pit of my stomach. I felt that my body was numb and paralyzed to the point where I couldn't feel the tears on my face. I lost full hope, and that I would lose my best friend who I called sister.

I asked her what did I do wrong, but before she could explain, she said bye and left the house in the game. I felt my heart melt. I teleported to Joselyn and asked, "Can you be my sister again?" She said yes, and I felt joy and was relieved. I said that I will never lose her again.

o O o

Zayden C.
age 6

In the Middle

I felt kinda in the middle about the party yesterday. We had cupcakes, sang happy birthday, went to the basketball court, and then I went home and slept. I felt in the middle because my shoe came off, and I got mud on my foot and shoes.

o o o

Zayla P.
age 8

My Cousin's House

When I was happy, I went to my cousins house. We had a grill. And we ate hot dogs and hamburgers, and it was good. Me and my cousin played hand games and hide and seek. We both took turns being the seeker. I hid in the bathroom shower, and they didn't find me for a long time. Later we watched the Secret Life of Pets 2. And it was good. And my cousin liked it too. It was the best day ever. And the house was big. And they were five rooms. And that's the end.

o o o

Zion S.
age 11

Relax!

I will tell you why I'm so relaxed because whenever I get mad, I take out my anger by ripping paper and playing soccer. I rip paper and play soccer to take out my anger because it helps me relax. Ripping paper will get me calm, and when I get mad I will want to kick things so I kick a soccer ball. That's why I'm so relaxed.

o o o

Zuri J.
age 8

The Best Day

Since you asked, I'll tell you why I'm so happy. I'm so happy because one day we were at soccer, and my brother was playing soccer. I like to watch him play. I like to watch him play soccer, because its enjoying, relaxing, and also I got to take a yummy snack —it was rice crispy treats covered in white chocolate.

I also got to play soccer with some kids and I also played with my mom's phone. (She did not unlock her phone, but I did pictures and videos after the soccer game). My two brothers and me got to go to the store to get candy, and when we got home, I got to talk to my best friend in the whole world.

After I talked to her for a couple minutes, we went to the Wildwood Park. It has a splash pad and splash park. When we got home, we ate a yummy dinner.

It was the finest day of my life.

o SAINT FLORIAN CASH CLUB o

From the Table to the World

Sitting down in a circle of friends,
like one big family, we lift each other
up with love & encouragement saying-

You are unlike the rest, but your mind is a gift unto this world,
bestowing a great inheritance unto the next generation by your existence.

So take this knowledge and go forth to be whatever you are called to be.
Be a lighthouse, be a river, be a rager, be a sauna, be an orchestral masterpiece, be a catalyst,
Be an extraterrestrial force of nature (and be good at it).   Just   BE!

Life frightens, but the moment you speak makes life tremble before you
and finally see that the words inside you are the beginning. Of everything.

Never forget the strength & power you have by sharing your story.
The world wants to strip you of color but you shall remain vibrant as rainbows after storms.
Remain vibrant, yes. And remember above all else you are loved. You are loved. You are loved.

-Kelsey, Ty, & Eileen

o SAINT FLORIAN CASH CLUB o

Anton T.
age 14

I Am

I am smart
I am black
I like to play games
video games are my favorite
video games are fun
I play by myself
I like watching movies
It makes me happy
Its calming
Im funny
Im a good friend

Choices

Video Games are like an adventure where you get to make all the choices. I love this because then I am in control like I have the power.

o o o

DeCaya R.
age 15

A Letter to Granny

Dear Granny,

I miss you! May 22nd, 2019, the day before my birthday you left me. It hurt me. I remember my sister coming into the den saying "Granny passed." I didn't believe it, but seeing my sister cry I knew it was true. Seeing my Auntie lower your casket made me burst into tears, but I had to see you again. Traveling to Mississippi to see you again really made the day because that was really my last time to see you. I had to wear sunglasses at your funeral, because I didn't want anyone to see me like that. I just wanted to see your bright smile and hear your beautiful loud laugh again. My heart shattered into pieces. Knowing you was gone. Knowing I won't be able to feed you again. When I fed you I would be like "Granny is it good," you would be like, "Yeah Mhmm." Knowing you won't be here to shout "freedom" while the fireworks are bursting into the air. Hearing you say, "Amen god," at every hour of the day. Hearing you talk about your "boyfriend" and your "car." Knowing you won't be in your room when I go to my cousin's house. I really miss you, thinking about you everyday. Just wanted to say I love you and I miss you o so very much.

Love your great granddaughter

o o o

Demoni R.

age 15

Granny

Honestly I don't know how to feel since you've left. My heart shattered into pieces since you've left the day before my birthday, May 22nd, 2019. You were caring, lovable, enjoyable, and a protector. We always made sure you were fed, clean, and smelling good. I remember when my sister came in the den and said, "Granny passed," and what she said hurt me. When we were on our way I was thinking about you the whole way there. I was not ready to see you like that and I was really not ready to see you get buried. I was thinking about you on the way back from Mississippi. I just wanna say that I love you and you will always have a special place in my heart. I also wanna say that everyone misses you and that we will come visit you soon.

○ ○ ○

Duane P.

age 15

Bugs

They scare the heck out of me.
I always feel like they're going to
jump out and kill me.
Any kinds of bugs
scare me. The only time
when I'm not scared is when I have my
shoes on, so I can step on them.
other than that super scared of
bugs.

Saint Florian

Elyjah M.
age 15

To E

No. No. You're not like more than 3 quarters of your own population. Your interests, they don't seem to... enter anyone else's mind, if they don't look at it the same way you do. No. No. Your dreams are anywhere else to where half the populations dreams are. No. No. You skin isn't going to match more than 97% of the skins you will see in the future you're choosing. Yes. Yes. You have potential, more than anybody you know. Yes, you are talented. Yes, you are beautiful. Yes, you are intelligent. Yes, you have things in your mind that nobody thinks you do. That's what makes you nobody else, and only you. Don't get distracted by earlier accomplishments, by people who doubted you. Your potential is off the charts man. Sexuality, interests, or skin color does not matter. Society will not steer you anywhere you don't want to be. The minority of minorities. One of a kind. How do you expect to have or even meet your own goals if you're too busy trying to meet somebody else's goals, Your DO NOT DISTURB sign is very showing to everyone that's your way of making your dreams come true. Stay strong and independent. In time everything will turn out to be in your favor. At this point, look up to yourself, if no one else. I love you. Keep making yourself happy.

○ ○ ○

Joniece L.
age 15

Truth

You wanna know my truth, the whole truth. The truth is I'm scared to let people know how I feel or what I feel. I'm scared to let people see who I really am as a person. I feel like the way I act, talk, walk and dress people will start to Judge me. I fear of falling in love, love hurts and I really just don't like that hurt feeling. I fear my inner self. Why? Because my inner self is just something I fear to show on the outside. I fear speaking up to people who talk about me or my friends. I fear that being bisexual my family and friends will turn their backs on me. I fear of death, I don't wanna know what death feel like. That's my truth my whole entire truth.

Jordan J.
age 15

Family Judgement

Family judgement. Why is this even a topic just off the bat? Family shouldn't judge family, they're supposed to be there in time of struggle in your worst days. When people turn their backs on you they're supposed to be there and tell you it's okay. One mistake can change peoples minds about you. This story isn't about me, this is about my oldest brother. He had scholarships from Texas State University and Florida A&M coming out of Pike High School. But one mistake changed the way people looked at him. One bad move and everyone lost faith in him, but that sit well with me. I promised never to forget him. The struggle is real from him. But how can I do that if he's family? They said don't answer the door if he comes. They said if he calls don't pick up. 28 years old with 5 children being a car mechanic. They won't let me see my nephews or nieces. They treat him like he's a stranger. But I promise, I promise one day when I get money and buy a house you got to stay in it. I promise I'm going to see my nephews and nieces. I promise to pull you out of the fight, the struggle, and pain. I won't and will never judge you.

○ ○ ○

Malena P.
age 14

Outside The Box

A lot of times people misunderstood me because I am different and I hate being stereotyped. When people stereotype you start to feel like you're stuck in one box. And a lot of times I start to feel like a slave to my mind because I'm basically stuck in one place and my grandmother always tells me to think outside the box but I feel like why-when there really shouldn't be a box… No one should have a say in my actions and what I want to do because this is my life that I'm living and I feel like I have the right to live my life to the fullest. And I'm fine with making my own mistakes along the way but I trust and love myself enough to know that no matter what situation may happen that can bring me down to my lowest falls, I know I have the strength to get up and not just on my own but also with my faith in God. Earlier in my life, I realized to not put my trust and faith in people because it's always the ones you trust the most who let you down. Not even the woman whose womb I was in for nine months can be trusted. So, it really sets a clear path in my mind that I have to do things on my own, but there's nothing wrong with a little help from others. But I know deep within my mind, but I know they won't be there for long and the love and support they once showed me will fade away, but it's okay because I'm prepared well enough to know that. God and myself are the only ones I can trust.

Sydney B.
age 15

Utter to my Granny

Dear Granny, my biggest fan, and best friend, my protector. This is the hardest thing I've ever had to overcome in my life due to the fact that you were always around me and never left me to be alone until May 22, you left me. You left our family. How all of us are missing you and your presence. Everything I do makes me miss you even more. I even hate sleeping because your room was right next to mine and I just have so many memories in that room. Like us watching Jumping The Broom and saying the girl was stupid for leaving the good man. I remember painting your nails and you would always call me and tell me about how people would say your nails were cute and you would tell them, "Oh my Sydney poo did them." You were such a vital person in my life. I miss you! I love you so much. I'm so mad at you that you didn't wait for me to be there in your final moments. But I'm also glad you're no longer in pain, or have to sit in a cold and boring hospital with people who are all dying and lifeless. You were still full of life on your worst days. I wish a form of you was still here so I could just hear you scream, "Amen God," out of nowhere. So I could hear you say, "Yes baby, I'm fine." You taught me how to love myself before loving others, to love the people who do you wrong. You taught me how to cook. You were truly like my second mom and I love you for everything. The talks, the jokes you always made about my head being big, making sure I was on the right path. You told me to love endlessly and to love hard. You will forever be here. I love you, and the ride has just begun! You believed having a good connection with God will always keep us connected. I've never really experienced a death this close to me before. I miss you more everyday! There were so many things we were supposed to do together. When you came home we were gonna throw you a party for getting out of the hospital! We were supposed to watch our favorite movie together. There are so many things your missing now. I love you.

Love, your granddaughter, Sydney

o o o

Counselor Nikki

Out of Place

The only one like you
The last of your kind
You're rare and new

It never fails that at some point I'll be the only one: why is that? It always makes me feel awkward...out of place
I shouldn't since I went to a predominantly white middle school
I feel like I shouldn't feel...out of place
Even in college most universities are Purl's
You could think I wouldn't feel...out of place
Thinking about it there aren't even a lot of black people in front of the kids at my job
One teacher is PHENOMENAL AND BLACK!
She is by far one of my favs
Not only because she's black but...she's an all around amazing human being
I'm jealous of our kids who get to experience her.
Maybe if I had a black teacher growing up I wouldn't have felt so...out of place at times
Even in coaching you don't see a lot of black faces
It seems like no matter where I'm at I'm...out of place
I hope one day that will change so future generations won't always feel...out of place.

Counselor Brandon

Penny Candy

The change in my pockets is weighing me down and all of them are Abraham Lincolns. Retrieved from mama's car seats, grandma's couch, and thatold purple bag that granddaddy used to own. You know the one with the yellow string and that was where every black child kept their money. I'm on my way to the penny candy store. You know that old ran down building that always sat on some number street or that old ladies house in the neighborhood that everyone went to. I remember stores like Bob's. Joe, Lee's, or some name that we all could relate to beacuse it was a black name. And all the candy inside the store wasn't the same, we had so much from which to choose. The girls on the candy wrapper we called Chews, Now n' Later with all types of flavors, Big Blows, Flamin' Hot Frito Lays, Air Heads, and to top it all off you know we had to get that 50 cent Faygo, where did those days go....
And I can remember my eyes getting so big as I poured all the change out counting each penny as the lady behind the counter who resembled my grandmother poured out all the candy in the brown sack and later on that evening we got some more change to come back.... I just wanted to take you back. Because today, I was feeling quite dandy. Because for some odd reason I had a sweet tooth for some penny candy.

○ ○ ○

HORIZONS AT SAINT RICHARD'S EPISCOPAL SCHOOL

The Horizons program at St. Richard's (SRES) is closing the achievement gap in Indianapolis by providing underserved children access to high-quality academics in an engaging program that primarily takes place in the summer, tuition free. Summer learning loss is the largest contributing factor to the national achievement gap putting low-income students as much as three years behind by the fifth grade.

In contrast, Horizons students, preK to 8th grade, gain an average of two to three months reading and math skills during the six-week summer program. In addition to preventing summer learning loss, Horizons has two other goals: increasing water safety by teaching children a life-saving skill through swim lessons at Butler University three times a week and obesity prevention by teaching and modeling healthy habits. Middle Division students and alumni are often assistants and mentors under direct supervision of the Horizons staff. Horizons is led by Executive Director Shanna Martin and Program Director Ashley Shufflebarger.

Composing Poetry at Horizons SRES

This year our third and fourth grade poets looked at poetry through the prism of their particular class theme. The 3rd grade theme "Engineering!" related well to the poet William Carlos Williams' assertion that "A poem is a (small or large) machine made of words." We considered how a poem is built of words derived through observation, imagination, and recollected memories. We engineered poems by asking questions, searching for sensory details, and collaborating. We invented new ways to express our emotions by making what's abstract concrete.

The theme for the 4th graders was "Healthy Minds, Healthy Bodies." To connect with that theme, we wrote odes to individual parts of our bodies and to a pair of shoes, either real or imaginary. We wrote an action-packed poem about a favorite physical activity and a list poem celebrating a beloved food. Gary Soto's book, Neighborhood Odes, provided us with some excellent, as well as assessible, models of celebratory poems.

Synergy sometimes occurred when what was learned during regular class time or on a field trip appeared in a poem. For instance, when a fourth grader wrote about why he liked apples, he compared the stem to "a blood vessel or a capillary," reflecting knowledge of the body gained during regular class time.

Sessions were fifty minutes long and usually began with reading the day's poetry prompt and a few models by professional poets, IWC interns, and even previous students. After we talked about the techniques that made these poems effective, we created a collaborative poem inspired by the prompt and then sat at tables to write individual poems. Interns and volunteers asked questions that helped the students develop ideas and images in more depth. For the last ten minutes of class, students volunteered to stand in front of the group to read their poems aloud.

I feel honored and blessed to have worked another year with the terrific students at Horizons and with my outstanding team of interns and volunteers. I hope you enjoy this sampling of poems from our workshop.

—Shari Wagner
Former Poet Laureate
Faculty Instructor
Building a Rainbow Youth Memoir Program
Indiana Writers Center Site

Alaya L.
age 9

My Glasses of Fear

When I wear these things, my glasses, I feel tight in a space. When they look at me in every trace, I find a thing to hide my face. The way they tease, the way they laugh, the way they see the real true person inside of me. I run and run and hide my face. The way I cry under the trees and mope and whine when they see my face. To see the bravery inside me, I walk down with my head up. God has taken my fear. God holds me in his arms and holds me tight and kisses me on the cheek. He tells me why they are so mean. Because they know not what's underneath--a fearless girl so brave, so strong, ready for action, powerful, peace of hope. He takes my glasses and breaks them in half and tells me I'm free from fear at last.

○ ○ ○

Brooklyn T.
age 9

California

Smells like roses and the wind goes in your hair. Their food tastes like the original California.   Hearing all the amazing sounds because all the good songs in California. Because of the cities you can see so good because of all the bright colors makes you will never want to leave.

○ ○ ○

Cecelia H.
age 10

The Trampoline

The trampoline is fun
2019: We love trampoline because we Jump, Everyday we can't stop

Christian A.
age 6

My Boots of Stupidity

Boots. Ugly, ugly boots.
Weigh10 pounds on your feet
Pull your feet from your ankles
Make you trip in front of your friends
Embarrassing, make me feel stupid
It's super loud when you run
on marble floor
They get dirty because they are so heavy
When they go on the ground
you can hurt your friends' toes
by stepping on them
All these boots make me feel stupid
because you step on your friends' shoes
They can beat you up
but you won't get in trouble
if it's an accident.
They are black and white
Red on the bottom
with blue and white stripes

Day'lee T.
age 9

The Shell

What could it be?
 A brown little shell every time I
flip it over
it is rumbly like an acorn but in a
shell as I put it up to my ear
it sounds like
wind blowing right in my ear
it might look scary
but i might disappear
it reminds me of a movie called
Moana
she blew and blew and blew until she could
not stop
It looks really smooth and feels really smooth
but when I pick it up I
 feel lots of slobber
As I look into the dots
I see a reflection of Africa

Devin R.
age 10

Jacket of Sadness

I'm sad when I'm wearing
my jacket, but I'm not sad when I'm
not wearing it. Blue as when I'm
crying. It's sad like when I don't have
a Tommy gun on Fortnite.
I'm sad when it's cold outside, and I
have to wear my jacket.

○ ○ ○

Donavin C.
age 10

Blue Jay Feather

Blue White Black
My favorite colors
The stripes remind me of
A blanket I got
On my seventh birthday

○ ○ ○

Ezra M.
age 10

Ode to the Legs

legs let you run
legs hold your feet
legs let you have fun
legs let you compete

you can play soccer, you can play tag
on my legs, you don't make me mad

are they springy? are they strong? look at my legs, they don't look wrong, oh my legs they are so long, nothing can go wrong.

Gyani H.
age 9

My Adidas Slides

They are black with three
White lines on the strap.
They are made of soft plastic
With the texture of a mouth guard.

They let me walk outside
Without putting on my shoes.
I can wear them to the store
So my feet won't be hot.
I can wear them after I wake up
So I don't step on Legos
I forgot to put away.

Harlem T.
age 9

Shoes of Joy

My shoes are cool At home
but I don't wear them in
school because it stinks my class
stink
The shoes are Jordan's
They are white and black
I wear them on weekends
when I go to skyzone
I feel comfortable
I feel lonely without my shoes
I don't run fast Without these shoes

○ ○ ○

Jahmir D.
age 10

An Ode to my Cheeks

you look like an oversized
burger bun, you help me chew my
food and hold all my food and
saliva and you help me
when I'm mad and you help
me during swim lessons

Jamia A.
age 10

Lemons

Why I love Lemons
It's an easy answer…
I love the taste
So sweet. So sour
The way they
Make my eyes water

I love how they're tangy

Jasohn S.
age 10

Calm Jazz

It helps me calm down
The sound of the saxophone
Is like the breeze of the ocean
Blue and green

The piano sounds like bees
Going to their home
Yellow and black

The trumpet sounds like an elephant
Blowing his horn
Gray

The trombone sounds like a lion
Roaring for prey
Brown and peach

The drum sounds like a Jamaican
Playing a bongo
Brown

Jeremiah T.
age 10

Why I Love Pizza

Because it's warm and cheesy
it tastes good with different toppings
like mushrooms, ham, black olives, and orange peppers
Because one time my family and I went to downtown
Indianapolis to a new pizza shop
it smells like pizza dough
it tastes like happiness
and it looks like my favorite shape

o o o

Jessyca C.
age 9

Pink Converse

Color pink lights me up whenever I see it. Helps me fly up in the sky. Laces keep me tied up from falling, They help me run like the wind. (Whoosh Whoosh)

o o o

Jonathan C.
age 9

Seashell

Feels soft and bumpy
Pointy in the top
Reminds me of going to the ocean
It comes from animals
It sounds like waves
Sand feels soft under my hand
The water is cold, full of fish

o o o

Joseph C.
age 9

My Coat of Fun

My coat of fun is orange and blue
It covers my arms with its long
Sleevs. Every time I wear it I have
A good time

Kameron J.
age 10

Earrings of Sadness

My earrings that I lost last year
Was a sad moment. The first earring
That I lost was when I was playing
With my brother and my cousin's husband's
friend's daughter, it was fun after that.
We went on the trampoline and I
Did 6 backflips and 6
front flips it
Was really really fun and then I left
And then I lost my earring and two
Months after that I threw that one
Because this boy took it out my ear on the
Bus

○ ○ ○

Kassidy B.
age 10

Friendship

Best friends are the
Ones who will pick
You up when no one
Notices you have fallen
That's what friends are for

Kendall S.
age 9

The Shell

It sounds like a flute or a piano.

It feels hard and bumpy.

There are different kinds of it.

It has all kinds of different shades of brown

o o o

Kyle M.
age 10

My Snow Boots

My snow boots are heavy as a rock
They are comfortable inside
even though they are small
my little feet are comfortable
Sometimes I jump in puddles
Sometimes I play in the rain
Sometimes I play in the snow from the sky
When there's a big snowy day
I can play in the snow
and shout "hooray!"
All my shoes are my friends
When I'm not wearing them
they look like they are talking
they say "put me on your feet".

Lauryn J.
age 9

Wasp Nest

It smells like toothpaste
It sounds like the paper cups
In a coffee maker

○ ○ ○

Ma'at D.
age 11

Talking Shoes

Talking shoes help people walk
Talking shoes can also talk
If you don't know where
to go, The Talking Shoes
can tell you where you
need to go. They're made
out of metal. Talking
shoes can make some
jokes, While they drink
coke. What would you
do if you had a talking
Shoe?

Maleik A.
age 10

Basketball

I like to play basketball I like to run
Around and shoot because I am fast
And because I like sports
I run as fast as lightning
I shoot as precise as art
When I play basketball in the heat
I need water to cool me down
Like the raindrops or twinkling stars
The basketball is shaped like a pear
Round and rock hard
It helps me concentrate

Marcus C.
age 9

The Hat of Anger

It is burning
It is trying to calm down
But it just can't
And every time I run past water
It gets more angry
At school everyone says
I just can't fit in
And then after school
This cloud just comes
And calms me down
The next day at school
Everyone wants to be my friend
Then my hat of anger
Saw another boy
And it calmed me down.
At night when he goes to sleep
He hears birds singing.

Ny'Asia A.
age 11

Lungs

Lungs make me feel like
I'm in the ocean when I relaxed
and they help me breath and stay
alive for another day, it kinda
feels like I am flying in the
sky so
high very high
    but my lungs are
        here so I won't
            die.

o o o

Paris P.
age 9

My Mouth

My mouth is filled with 24 teeth
All my teeth white. And my mouth
Is for talking singing eating. And my
Hands are for Writing and Math.
and my legs are for running. My eyes are
For seeing things like my mom, my
Dogs.

Quinnija T.
age 10

My Ear

You make me hear cause you're my EAR you make
Me hear everything and you love wearing earrings
and I only put it in when I count to 1-2-3 you shine
Like a diamond and the sky I wish I can tell you why
I like dressing you up everyday no matter what you
Say I know I don't play with you a lot but
My dad will and it will always do that.
I can't hear nothing without you look like
You will always be with me and I will always
Be with you.

o o o

Quintarius T.
age 9

Fire of Anger

Everytime I think of it, I burn.
It is red and blue
Everytime I think of it, I burn in
My shoes.
I get so mad it burns my ears
And makes me go in tears

Romeo C.
age 9

The Sunglasses of Happiness

When I wear my sunglasses
I feel like a new man
I look beautiful
I see darkness
Like Batman
And the light is not that bright
But when I look at
The sun, the sun is too
Bright for me it's
Like I'm it
Sometimes I wear it
Because I want to

Summer O.
age 9

My Shoes

My shoes are dirty
Because people are stepping
On them
My shoes are colorful
Like the rainbow
My shoes are made
Of knitted cotton
I like that you can do
Anything in them
Like run in them
Jump in them
Climb in them
They take me to the store
And to the gas station
When I go to sleep
They get kicked
By my sisters

Sydney S.
age 10

Volleyball

Me and my teammates
Play volleyball
Our parents cheer us on
Yelling hit that ball over
The wall score your
Team a point SMACK there goes
The ball over the net but we haven't
Won the game yet

Thomas M.
age 9

Eagle Creek Boats

There was one people boats
There was two people boats
There was four people boats
They were short
There was eight people boats
They were long
There was silver boats
There was one wooden one
There was black ones
There was yellow ones
There was red ones
There was white ones
There was blue ones
Some boats were used for racing
I learned how to measure them
There were old ones
We moved the boats to see them
And see how they move
And what they look like
There were two 58 foot ones
There was one that was 13 feet
There was one that was 17 feet
There was one that was 25 feet
The boats were amazing

Ulysses L.
age 10

Basketball

Basketball is fun
I play with my friends
I play on teams
We win
We lose
I have trash players
I have good players
I have good sportsmanship
I'm not a sore loser
I'm not a sore winner
The basketball is puffy
The basketball is fluffy
I like 23 Jordans

Zaniah W.
age 10

Ode to my Eyes

You help me see pictures and you help me watch TV and you help me see in the night and the day time and you help me see my dog and play with him.

3rd Graders Collaborative Poem

Why We Liked Our Fieldtrip to the Arcade

Because of the games,
Their screws and levers.
Because we heard the burrr
And skrrrr and ding dong
Of racing games, shooting games,
And basketball games.
Because of the prizes—
Candy, bags of balloons,
And 100-piece puzzles.
Because we took pictures
At the photo booth,
Three friends at a time.
Because of the food
We smelled from downstairs—
Chinese food, tacos, and pizza.
Because when we went outside
we saw a parking lot
with a wishing well.
Because we put our fingers
in the water.
Because we made a wish.

4th Graders Collaborative Poems

Our Horizons Poetry Shoes

Make us shoes that walk up trees
To get a bird's-eye view.
Make us shoes that jump to the moon.
Make us shoes that climb up
Twisty-turn slides.
Make us shoes that run like a cheetah
To Alaska and back.
Make us shoes made with bubbles
Like Air Max shoes
And bubbles floating in the sky.
Make us shoes that talk
When the heels click.
Make us shoes that play music.
Make us shoes that dance.

Why I love Mandarin Oranges

Because they're orange
like the sunset
or a sunflower
Because they're shiny
with a bit of green
Because they smell like
oranges and pinecones
Because they taste
wet and delicious
Because I ate a mandarin
last week for lunch
with a friend
Because they give me
Vitamin C
to keep away a cold.

Ode to My Ear

You're shaped like an oval upside down,
a moon, a pear, a butterfly.
You help me hear people talking,
roller coasters with a chug-chug train sound,
and my favorite songs.
You help me hear shells in the ocean
and the TV.
You're a shelter for my hair.
You're a little brother to my head.
You shine with earrings
that glitter like diamonds.

We Love Swimming at Horizons

Because on a hot day, we swim at the JCC
where the water is cold and gives us goosebumps
Because we like to dive in and splash
like dolphins, seals, sharks and mermaids
Because of the fast waterslides
Because we backstroke and do somersaults
Because we swim like a puppy
Because it smells like chlorine and the ocean

WESTMINSTER YOUTH SERVICES SUMMER PROGRAM

Students in the Westminster Youth Services Summer Program enjoy a wide range of activities that encourage learning and healthy lifestyles, such as swimming lessons, trips to local libraries and participation in summer reading programs, exploring local nature preserves, physical fitness, nutrition, and healthy cooking classes, gardening time, and other enriching activities.

Each Monday and Wednesday we were lucky to join the young writers at Westminster as they explored their own thoughts and ideas and shared their stories with us. Writers between the ages of five and sixteen clambered into the room chatting and laughing, some eager to find out what the prompt of the day would be, others worrying aloud that they would have nothing to write about: but, of course, they always had something to say, something to write down, something they were paper-raised-high-in-the-air-eager to share.

And, we, the writer/teacher/scholars charged with facilitating their writing experience, were always amazed. Sure, we made plans. We developed prompts we thought would help them catch just a little bit of the poetry that they played and joked and danced around the room with into a written format that could be shared with others. And, for some, these carefully planned prompts worked marvelously. They sat quiet and still, thinking about what they might say about their homes or the things and people they love, or the things and people that made them angry or afraid, and then they wrote and wrote and wrote.

For others, when the prompts failed to pull them in, they preferred to talk, joke, laugh, or even sing. And, without fail, leaving just a little space open to allow them to do these things, stretch their voices in the ways they saw fit led them back to the page.

The result of this, of leaning into and meandering away from the planned program with the assurance that we wanted nothing from them but their authentic selves is that they always came back to us and back to what was really important: their stories unfiltered and unfettered.

—Ashley Mack-Jackson
Faculty Instructor
Building a Rainbow Youth Memoir Program
Indiana Writers Center

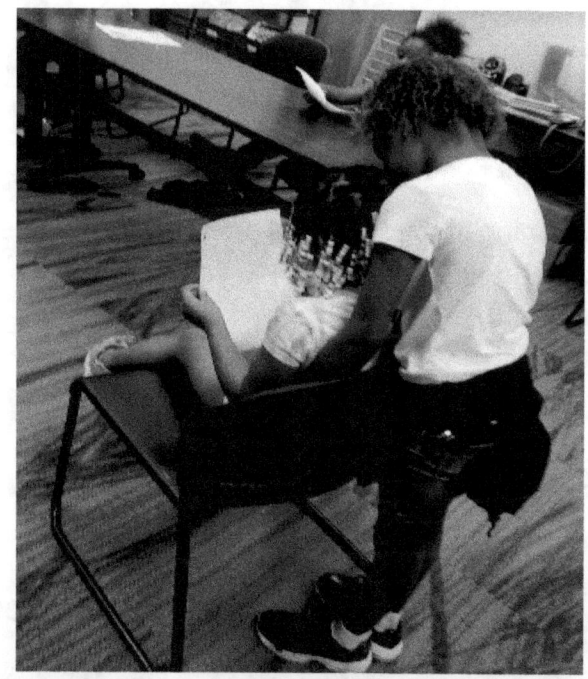

Alex W.
age 9

Taking a Dip

I like to go swimming in the summer. I wear my green Minecraft trunks in the pool. I go swimming with my grandma. I hate sunscreen.

○ ○ ○

Angel H.
age 9

A Buffet Like No Other

When I walk into Golden Corral, I see a menu wall. We get a tray and pay and we get drinks. When we got there, I ate steak and mashed potatoes and corn. This smells good. It was chewy and the mashed potatoes was squishy, and it was so good. And for dessert, I eat ice cream brownie, and marshmallow. When I got the steak, it was medium rare and it smell good and taste good.

○ ○ ○

Ava K.
age 9

Meeting My Best Friend

Her name is Mackenzie. She has dirty, blonde hair. She only wears black leggings and black shorts. And love to wear crop tops. And she loves makeup. We meet at daycare. First I was playing, and I felt a whack and turned and Mackenzie was laughing. We were jumping off the play set, and she fell and got up and fell back down in a dramatic way. She is my best friend because she is caring.

Breayre P.
age 8

A Whale of a Time at the Beach

One summer day, I went to the beach and I played in the sand, played in the water, ate lunch, and a bird tried to get my food. I went with my auntie and my cousins and my sister. And I played gymnastics in the sand. I made a big sandcastle\. It was sunny outside, very sunny. I got shells. And took a nap. I stick my head in the water.

○ ○ ○

Cristina B.
age 10

I Didn't Order a McDouble!

McDonald's has a big menu. It also smells like french fries. I don't like the tomatoes, but I really like their french fries and drinks. I also see so many people in McDonald's. When the cashier opens the register, I want all the money. There are so many people in line, it looks like a packed hut. It looks like a game where you have to run into people and make them get in your group. The people in there also smelled funky. When I walked into McDonald's and they took my order, they took about five minutes, and they came back and called my order. I was supposed to get one bag, but they gave me two, I didn't say anything because I was hungry. They doubled my order! I eat it and I was full. I was with my mom on a Sunday afternoon on a sunny day. I got a ten piece nugget, medium french fries, a Coca-Cola, and a cookie.

○ ○ ○

Dalilah C.
age 7

The Great Worm Chase

My sister made me mad because she kept chasing me with dirt that was muddy and it had a big fat worm. I started running fast and my sister was going slow. I ran to go tell my mom because she kept doing it over and over. My mom told Lindsey to go to her room. Then I was happy that my sister got in trouble.

○ ○ ○

David A.
age 11

Racism

Hello, my name is David, and I want to bring up racism. So, the two people I think have a big history with racism are Donald Trump and Hitler. Donald Trump wants to get rid of all the Mexicans. Hitler wanted to get rid of the Jews. Donald Trump tried to block the Mexicans from coming to the United States of America. But he failed. Hitler wanted to kill all the Jews. But he failed too. They both failed because we worked together to stop them. If we work together we can end racism for good. That is why we need to continue fighting racism, to end it for good.

○ ○ ○

De'niyah J.
age 10

Loving Myself

I like the way I dress. I like that I'm a good dancer. I make up some dances. Lots of people think I'm funny, and I like that too. I do all types of pranks. I also make friends quick, so I am friendly. My friends depend on me. I'm a leader, not a follower. I love Westminster. I'm an artist. I also like to paint, draw. My art is colorful, nice, and pretty. Me De'niyah is very respectful and responsible. I sing very well and I practice rap music. And I really like watching YouTube. I like my first day of the Writer Center. I like I'm a good writer.

○ ○ ○

De'lilah J.
age 12

At My Cousin's House...

Hear: Quiet and music hip hop and bang pots and pans

See: TV What playing YouTube and baby cuz and cuz and me and we dance

Smell: Candy and grass

Taste: Cakes (Jen cake) and pizza (cheese)

Feel: Kisses and hugs and tables

○ ○ ○

De'mone S.
age 7

To De'lijah

The most important person in my life is my big brother De'lijah. He play with me all the time. He play all the games. We play basketball together. He is nice. He is 13.

○ ○ ○

De'lijah J.
age 13

In Nowhere

Fun, bored, and hear nothing, can taste nowhere, I feel nowhere, I see walls, no floor, and I am flying, and it's fun to fly. It was fun. I have wings, and I can fly anywhere and do anything at nowhere and my room.
Spitting Bars Like Snoop Dogg
I am funny, and I like candy, and I am creative. Others think I'm funny and good at roasting. I rather be like Snoop Dogg, because he is funny— although I am funnier than him. I also like to spit bars and rap like Snoop Dogg.
Dontrell J., age 15
Follow the Leader
My mom's baby daddy came to our house and went in my room and opened my window and just jumped out the window and landed on his feet. Then the rest of the cousins saw him do it, and they started doing it. When I wanted to do it, my mom grabbed me and yelled at me for trying to do it.
After she left to go to the store, I did it since nobody saw me and my whole family was out and they didn't even let me do it.

○ ○ ○

Doran P.
age 12

Protector

I felt proud of who I am when I stood up for my little brother and little sister. We were at the park and two little girls were throwing mulch on them. I went up to them and told them to stop throwing mulch at my siblings. They finally stopped when I told them. I felt proud because I am the big brother and I like to always protect them.

○ ○ ○

Elijah W.
age 10

I Love My Mom

The most important person in my life is my mom. Because she keeps a roof over my head. She keeps clothes on my back. And shoes on my feet. She wants us to have a better history than what she had. And she protects me. She would do whatever she could to protect me.

The best memory of my mom is when it was her first ever perfect birthday. She loved her birthday. She invited her friends over and her friends had kids their kids were over friends and they were fun to play with. They never messed up the house. If they did, we would have cleaned it up. Just for the sake of my mom.
I love my mom more than anything. I would do anything for my mom to stay safe. She is fun to play with. She loves us. I'm pretty sure that she loves us. She is the best mom I can imagine. She would never abandon us. And I know that she would and can dance if she got a free million dollars.
She is a little childish. And sweet, sweeter than a piece of candy. And she changed my world a lot. She shares stuff with me I probably wouldn't make it this far without her. And probably wouldn't be writing this if it wasn't for her.
I Love my mom.

Gustavo H.
age 8

Friends at the Park

I was with Mr. Seth and Park and did activities outside and inside, and we played basketball. It is not about winning it is about having fun and to getting to know each other.

Hayven B.
age 11

It Wasn't a Dare

I drank a mix of cottage cheese, fruit, hot sauce, and strawberry milk.
A few days later, I chugged a small packet of hot sauce and refused to go to the nurse. I was bored and my friends were trying to take the ten hot sauce packages I had away from me. It tasted like water, but if you put a ghost pepper in it. My throat burned for four days. I refused to go to the nurse but I didn't go because the nurse doesn't do anything. :-P

Jacobi N.
age 13

My Resilient Dog, Cino

My dog is my best friend. His name is Cappuccino, but we call him Cino. We found him in St. Louis at my younger cousin's school. They had a small fence around the school, and he was curled up in a ball and shaking.

My dad saw him and stopped. We had hotdogs in the car for some reason. He took one out and tried to feed it to him, but he didn't want to eat. My dad picked him up and put him in the car. Since we found him, we didn't know what kind of dog he was, but by the way it was a male. But since we didn't know what he was, we started guessing from the shape of his head that he was a Pitbull but because of his height, we assumed he was mixed with something.

We've had him for four or five years, but during those years he became more like a human. If you're laying down, he will stand next to you really quietly in a menacingly way until you let him under your covers. He also demands that you share your pillow. But some bad things have happened to him since we had him. About one or two years after we got him, he got hit by a car, and he refused to let us bandage his leg because it was broken—but it healed fine. About last year, he was shot twice, once in the face and once in the leg. It went through his back leg into his front left leg.

He survived, but the vet said his left leg needed to be amputated. We couldn't afford it so we didn't amputate it. He learned to walk without putting too much weight on it, but the pain eventually subsided. Now the only time he limps is when he hits his paw on something.

○ ○ ○

Jada F.
age 10

Toilet Bowl Water Slide

My favorite day of the summer is when I went to King's Island, when I went to the water park. In the water park, we went on a so called ride. It went down so fast, I could not even breathe for 10 seconds. There were three tubes on this so called ride, the tubes were blue and smelled like chlorine. We went on this toilet the size of the building and even maybe bigger so we had a floatie. That was fun. Me and my mommy and my cousins got on it, and we went SWISH!! It was amazing and at the end there was a big pool. Also another place in the water park ,it was like an ocean with the waves and lights. We had the big pool to ourselves.

o o o

James L.
age 7

Let Me Introduce You to Lindsey

Lindsey is the best. And she always care for me even though I care for her. And that is she is cute and smart and funny. You play all day, like tag. We always play together because we're friends. I met her at the park.
We were running around and playing on the monkey bars and played mom and dad, and she was the sister, and I was the brother. And we played babysitter too.
And she's always the best. And she's the funniest in the whole wide world. And we also played "get revenge on the stuff that attacks us." Lindsey likes to be with her sister sometimes ,which is alright because we always play together.
We play together at the park and the gym, and the only time we don't is when we go home and we're alone. And we also took a drink and like went to the barn and saw pigs. They were so cute! And the baby cat, and mommy cat and Lindsey was trying to keep up with me so we can throw rocks, even big ones, in the lake. And also she's the only biggest best friend of mine. And that's it.

Jayden B.
age 10

A Little About Myself

What I like about myself is my personality. People say I have a beautiful eye color. I'm a smart kid, and I have great teachers, like Ms Ashley, Ms Emily, Mr. Jeff, Mrs. Jen, Ms Nykasia, Mr. Ty, Ms Cassie, and more. I love Westminster. But I don't care if people say I have a bad style. I think I have a good style, and I'm a good kid, people say to me sometimes. I love my personality. I love my middle names Christopher Roger. I am nice and I respect people. I think I have a great personality, and I can do the worm, and I can stand on my head and spin. I am awesome in my own way. So that is what I like about myself. What do you like about yourself?

○ ○ ○

Keiyon S.
age 10

Those Who Love Me Most

Family: My family does everything in their power to keep me safe. They make me proud of myself and they make me believe in myself. They help me with everything I need. They spend what they can on me. My family is a role model to me. They reach out for me. They turn my life into a good one. Thanks to my family.

○ ○ ○

Kinesha P.
age 8

Cutie the Cat

My best friend is my cat. Her name is Cutie. She was a kitten when I got her from my mom's friend. I was very excited that I got to hold her. She is a furry grey cat with brown eyes. When she came inside my house, she walked around my living room. Then we gave her milk and cat food. When she was finished eating she cuddled in my bed with me. When we got up the next morning we at breakfast. I was able to give her a bath in the sink.

Lindsey C.
age 6

James and I

My best friend is James. He has blonde hair and blue eyes. I met him at his first day of camp. We played at the park. We got on the monkey bars and swings. We love to play tag and color. We see each other every day so we always have fun. Sometimes we play babysitter. James is always nice to me and he is funny! We like to tell jokes. Together we are very funny. When we go to the gym we play with the balls and play games. Our favorite field trip together was at the farm. We saw baby pigs, cats, dogs, and birds.

Major F.
age 5

My Brother Keeps Bugging Me

My brother Randall was chasing me with a worm. And my mom said, "Stop!" And he stopped, and told me I'm lucky. And then the other day he said he'd put a spider and worm on me in my sleep because I don't like spiders and worms. But he didn't, because he was being nice to me. He tried to get me close to a spider to drop it on me, and I said hurry up so I can step on it, and he did, and I ran to a spiky bush that pricked me like the ones at my pawpaw's house. So he didn't let me play with the lightning bugs even though we were looking for them, and he wouldn't let me go catch some, because he didn't want no stranger to get me.

○ ○ ○

Mykell J.
age 5

My House

I hear…
a cat meow
a dog is barking
a bird is chirping

I see…
three red roses
a tree and also a lightning bug

I smell…
chocolate chip cookies
my house smells like sprite

I taste…
a turkey sandwich with mayo, lettuce, and that's all
vanilla ice cream with rainbow sprinkles

I feel…
itchy because there are a lot of mosquito bites **
soft blankets and they are comfortable

Natalia F.
age 12

Revenge & Cheez-its

So one afternoon I was sitting at the table, I had a bowl of Cheez-Its, and my brother was sitting by me. And we were eating our Cheez-its, and the kitchen led into the dining room and I could see the TV through the doorway. My favorite movie was on, Tinker Bell, so I was eating and watching the movie at the same time. I look over to watch the movie for a little bi,t and when I turned around, I heard some rustling and I thought it was my mom because she was in the kitchen cooking dinner. But when I turn around and looked into my bowl, and I notice I have less Cheez-Its than I had before.
So I look around. First I thought I had just ate too many, but then I was like, "No I didn't." I look at my mom, she was cooking, so she couldn't have done it. Then the exact name pops up in my head "Randall," my brother. So I just had to investigate. I looked in his bowl when he wasn't looking, and I sneakily grab the Cheez-It box and smack him in the head repeatedly to get my revenge. So I look over and my Mom's just cracking up and then I start to laugh too. But Randall was crying, but I didn't care. And I also ate the rest of his Cheez-Its. The End.

○ ○ ○

Navaeh F.
age 14

Swinging Finger

I was four at the time and just playing with my little brothers and sister by the door. Then the next thing later, she close the door on my finger. I screamed and cried. Then she opens it, then I get scared, because I see my bone, and then it starts to swing. I h ran down the stairs. I told my grandma, and she immediately took me to the sink to rinse it off and then called 911. When I got into the ambulance, they ask me if I wanted a crayon. I sad no at first, but then when we got to the hospital, I said yes. My mom worked at the hospital that I went to. When we got there they put some ice on it. Then some doctors came in to help put it together.

Obiora (Obi) O.
age 13

The Gym is Home

I feel at home when I am in the gym. The gym is where I play basketball. When I am in the gym, I hear basketballs dribbling, and people playing on teams, yelling about what to do with the ball and where to go with the ball. I see people playing basketball and pushing, shoving, turning, twisting, and doing tricks to get the ball in the net. I smell sweaty shoes and smelly bodies, but it is a good thing. I feel happy and sweaty, hot and hurt.

○ ○ ○

Randall F.
age 11

Touchdown & Tears

I don't really have a most important person, but since my mom and dad are still together/married, they are one. They are the most important because first of all, I would not be here, they pay for me and all my siblings, and they help me. We do so much fun stuff together. We go to King's Island play and sometimes, I get in trouble. Sometimes me and my dad go outside and condition (for football). My most favorite memory with my dad is my first touchdown. I was 8 years old and I took off my gloves cuz in warm up, I was missing the passes (we were at Butler University), so then I was wide open, burnt my many, I'd ran 22 yards, then caught it and made the touchdown.
It made my dad cry, so he threw his water bottle on himself. I asked why he was wet, and he said he was sweaty. Later in the car, he said he cried and that's why he poured water on himself.

Richard (RJ) G.
age 11

My Cousin Jayden

My cousin Jayden is my best friend because he is a cool, nice, caring, and loving kid, and he is the best ever. That's why he is my best friend, and he is a cool cousin to have as a best friend. I have known Jayden my whole life. I play with him we play on each others games. We also play in the pool. My favorite thing to do with him is jumping on the trampoline and playing basketball.

○ ○ ○

Samarei M.
age 6

At Home

At Home
I hear big green toy dinosaurs and my mom call my name, "Samarei."
I see black cars and blue hoverboards.
I smell burgers with cheese, lettuce, and mayo. Also fried chicken wings.
I taste glazed crispy bacon and fruity gummy bear candy.
I feel happy emotions and good feelings.

Juju
Juju is my best friend. He is five years old. He is black with long back hair. We met at the park, and we started to play with each other. W played hide and go seek, freeze tag, and we went to the water park together. We've been best friends for a long time. He's got a big brother and his big brother is named Jarell and he's got a mom and his mom's name is Natalia. She works with a doctor. I like Juju because he's fun, and I get to play with him often. We always go to the park. He's a good friend.

Samya R.
age 8

Family First

The first important person is my family. They are the best because I like going out to eat with them. And sometimes I like going swimming with them. And I like going on trips with them. And I like dancing. And I like sleeping with my family. And my family is tall and big and small.

○ ○ ○

Saniy R.
age 9

A Heart for Mom

My best friend is my mom. She loves elephants. She loves wearing jewelry. She's beautiful. She is a hair stylist. She like going swimming. When we went on vacation, we were riding in our car, and she was screaming. I was laughing. She was screaming, because she didn't know where she was going. My two siblings was with me and my cousin. She is my best friend because I love her and she loves me.

○ ○ ○

Shelia G.

age 12

Butterfly

My best friend is my dog, and her name is Butterfly, and she is cute, little, funny, nice, yappy, and lovable. She is a Mini Pinscher, and she is half-blooded, and she very little, and she is black and tan. I got her at my grandpa's tire shop and got her from my Uncle Timmy when she was five years old, and I was five years old. Now I'm 12 years old, and she is too. And when I got her from my Uncle Timmy, he was selling her, and I seen her so I had to get her, and I look at my mama and daddy, and I asked them, "Could I have her?" and they said yes. And, I was so happy, but now she is all grown up, and I am her owner, but she loves my mama so much that she thinks my mom is her owner. But yeah that is all about my best friend, that is my dog, and I love her to death.

My Home is Home

My home is home and it is quiet and loud sometimes. My house is fun and boring and my Mama make some fire food and it feels warm.

o o o

Stephan B.

age 12

Because He treats Me Well

Jacobi he goes to Westminister; he is really funny. He is good at Uno and at Slap Jack, and that's funny because his nickname is Jack. When we are on the playground, he spins me in these spiner things, and he spins me really fast. Also he's nice to me when I see him. His dog's birthday is also his birthday. I can win against him in Go Fish and in Spoons so that's cool. I have known him for a year now, and he is really fun to hang around with. This is all about why he is my friend, but mostly the part when I said he is nice to me because he was the one who was nice to me in the first place. His dog's name is the name of a coffee.

Toniah M.
age 7

May 7th Birthday

We are swimming and playing games. And then we get out of the pool and eat cake. Chocolate! We eat cake because it was my birthday. There were presents. My favorite present was a doll. And we played games inside the house. We played Limbo, and then we played Jenga. We played Twister. We went in the house, and I blew my candles out on the cake. There were 7 candles. And I had a lot of fun.

○ ○ ○

Troy T
age 12

Family Practice

My mom was practicing notes with me, and my dad was playing with me. It was hot at my game because I was practicing all day. I'm not on a team, but I play baseball with my family.

○ ○ ○

Tyiana M.
age 8

No Place Quite Like Home

I hear quiet and chirping. I see my toys, action figures and houses, and my brother's car. I see my mom cooking sometimes, like cookies and lots of sweets. I smell perfume because my sister's always usin' perfume and doin' makeup tutorials. Our home is big. I taste chicken wings! They're crispy! And mashed potatoes! I feel my slime. Purple and pink.

Zoey S.
age 6

Being A Big Sister

My favorite person is my baby sister, she is a newborn. She's adorable. Her name is Autum. I like to play Peek a Boo with her. If you tickle her under her arms, she'll smile. When she was born, I had to put hand sanitizer on before I could hold her. At first I didn't know my mom was having a baby. I wanted a baby sister so bad and I said, "Mommy, Mommy! Can I hold her?" and mom said "Yes." Every time I kiss her on the cheek she laughs, and she pulls my hair.

○ ○ ○

Zyllah L.
age 8

I Like Me

My best qualities:

- Style
- I am not nice; I like me
- I don't like glitter; I like me
- I don't like colors; I like me

I like me because I don't like nothing but me. I like my hand. I don't like colors because they sit there. I like my brain because it makes my hand sit there.

APPENDICES

WRITING PROMPTS

Below find the writing prompts for each of the three unique sites we served. We share these prompts with you in the hopes that you will join our community of writers and write your own stories.

Saint Florian JC and Core or Littles and Middles

- Tell me a story about a time when you stopped believing it would get better.

- Tell me a story about a time when you believed it would start to get better.

- Since you asked, I'll tell you why I'm so.... (angry, worried, scared, hopeless, fearful, hopeful, happy, etc...)

- Tell me the story of what happened when someone was cruel to you or made you feel less than you are because of the color or your skin or what you look like, where you live, go to school, or maybe even who your family is.

- Tell me the story of what happened when someone made you feel proud of who you are or lifted you up.

- Tell me a story about a time when you felt total content with no worries.

- Tell me the story about a time when you felt tough and brave.

- Describe a scar you have on your body. Tell me the story of how you got it.

- Describe your favorite pair of shoes and tell me the story about something that happened when you were wearing them.

- Tell the story about what happened when you lost something important to you.

- Tell the story about what happened when you lost someone important to you.

Saint Florian CASH Club

*NOTE: All the prompts were given to the students at the beginning of our time together. They were allowed to pick a prompt to focus on in any capacity they chose. Each day we met we spent a little bit of time focusing on a particular prompt, but we left the writing topics open to shift and change as the conversation ebbed and flowed.

Speak Your Mind

Activist Maggie Kuhn said, "Stand before the people you fear and speak your mind -- even if your voice shakes. When you least expect it, someone may actually listen to what you have to say. Well-aimed slingshots can topple giants."

Imagine this: You have 2 minutes to tell the whole world your truth. For 2 whole minutes, everyone in the world will stop, listen and be completely open to what you have to say. What is your truth that you want to share with the world? What do you feel passionately about? What moves you? What's on your mind? Leave your fear behind and tell us your truth.

Life Doesn't Frighten Me At All

Poet Maya Angelou wrote the following words in her poem, "Life Doesn't Frighten Me at All":

I've got a magic charm
That I keep up my sleeve
I can walk the ocean floor
And never have to breathe.

Life doesn't frighten me at all
Not at all
Not at all.

Life doesn't frighten me at all.

What scares you? Write a poem to speak out against and negate that fear. You are the best hype-person you'll ever know. There's no one else who can encourage you like YOU! Speak life to yourself. Hype yourself up.

___

The Day You Begin

In her children's book, The Day You Begin, Jacqueline Woodson writes, "There will be times when you walk into a room and no one there is quite like you. Maybe it will be your skin, your clothes, or the curl of your hair...This is the day you begin to find the places inside your laughter and your lunches, your books, your travel and your stories, where every new friend has something a little like you--and something else so fabulously not quite like you at all."

Time passes and things change, but there is only one you. Write an anthem to yourself today or write an anthem to yourself ten years from now. What do you want to say to yourself today? What do you want to say to your future self?

___

Young, Gifted & Black

The great singer-songwriter Nina Simone sang, "To be young, gifted and black/Is where it's at."

What does it mean to be black? What are the joys? What are the hardships and sorrows? Is it rewarding? Was Nina right? Tell us where it's at.

Horizons at Saint Richard's Episcopal School: Poetry Prompts

A Poem About a Family Member
Write a poem that creates a portrait of someone in your family who is important to you

An Object Poem
Write a poem about the object in your grab bag—a poem that helps us see that object in new and interesting ways. First observe the object closely by using your senses and then employ your imagination to create comparisons and to describe what it would be like to be this object.

A List Poem
Write a poem listing all the different reasons why you love your favorite place

My Necklace of Anger
Choose one of your emotions (fear, joy, sadness, hope, loneliness, etc.) and invent an article of clothing or an accessory that's designed to express that emotion in all kinds of ways! Make this article of clothing seem real and magical through your descriptive words and comparisons.

My Earrings of Happiness
Choose one of your emotions (fear, joy, sadness, hope, loneliness, etc.) and invent an article of clothing or an accessory that's designed to express that emotion in all kinds of ways! Make this article of clothing seem real and magical through your descriptive words and comparisons.

Writing Haiku
Today you will be creating several three-lined poems called haiku. First, look closely at what is around you. What catches your interest? What do you see, hear, smell, or touch? How one thing remind you of something else?

Westminster Neighborhood Services

- Tell the story of your most perfect summer day ever. Describe a place that you love and tell the story of something that happened there.
- Tell the story about what happened when something or someone made you really mad.
- Describe the most important person in your life. Why are they so important to you?
- Tell the story of a time when you felt tough and brave
- Describe your best friend. Tell the story of how you became friends.
- Write about your best qualities or what you like most about yourself. Tell me a story about a time when you felt proud to be who you are.
- Tell me the story about what happened when you lost something or someone important to you.
- Tell me the story of your best day ever.
- Tell me about what happened when you had to do the hardest thing in your life.
- Describe a memorable place where you've been. Tell the story of what happened in that place.
- Tell me the story about what happened when you did something that you later felt sorry about.
- Describe your most memorable holiday. Tell the story of what happened on that day.
- Describe a time that you were cruel to someone or someone was cruel to you. If you could go back to that time, what would you do differently?
- Write a letter to your future self. Do you have anny regrets to apologize for? What are the dreams and goals that you're most excited about? What advice do you have for yourself?

EDITOR AND DESIGNER BIOGRAPHIES

Dr. Darolyn "Lyn" Jones serves as the Education Outreach Director for the Indiana Writers overseeing the Building a Youth Public Memoir Program. Lyn is also an assistant teaching professor in the Department of English at Ball State University. Lyn is passionate about literacy, story, and social and educational justice and has committed her twenty-seven years of professional life to those topics. She is the educational author of a top selling series book titled Painless Reading Comprehension, co-author of Memory Workshop with Barbara Shoup, the editor for a digital literary magazine, Rethinking Children's & YA Lit: Read for Change, an editor for the children's book series, the Neon Tiki Tribe, and one of the editors of this independent press, INwords Publications. Lyn has edited and published multiple essays and memoir collections including Monday Coffee and Other Stories of Mothering Children with Special Needs, Where Mercy and Truth Meet: Homeless Women of Wheeler Speak, "Sitting at the Feet of my Flanner House Elders: A Lesson After Dying," and seven volumes of I Remember: Indianapolis Youth Write about Their Lives. Read more about Lyn's work and follow her blog at www.thelynjones.com.

Andrea Boucher has more than twenty years of professional experience in every facet of book design and publishing. She is the principal book designer for Indiana Writers Center and Butler University's literary journal Booth. Andrea holds an MFA in Creative Writing from Butler University.

Eileen Porzuczek is currently a graduate student at Ball State University studying Emerging Media Design and Development. Previously, she graduated with a BA in English, concentration in creative writing, and a minor in professional writing and emerging media from Ball State Univeristy. Eileen has worked with the Indiana Writer's center for the past three summers on their Buiilding A Rainbow Summer Program. She has also worked as a writer, editor, and designer for the digital magazine Rethinking Children's & YA Lit. Eileen has also worked as a designer for The Broken Plate and has a background inCorporate/Nonprofit Public Relations.

ACKNOWLEDGEMENTS

The Indiana Writers Center's Building a Rainbow Youth Public Memoir Program gratefully acknowledges the support of these organizations and individuals for their contributions and time.

Executive Director
Rachel Sahaidachny

Writer in Residence
Barbara Shoup

Education Outreach Director
Darolyn "Lyn" Jones

Site Instructors
Ashely Mack-Jackson, Barb Shoup, Emily Mack, Shari Wagner

Book Design & Layout Team
Andrea Boucher and Eileen Porzuczek

Lead Teaching Intern
Cassidy Langston

University Teaching, Editing, and Public Relations Interns
Hannah Eadie (BSU), Devon Lejman (BSU), Ty Johnson (UIndy), Sydney Jordan (BSU), Cassidy Langston (BSU Alum), Maria Piazzzo, Dillon O'Nail (BSU), Eileen Porzuczek (BSU Alum), Megan Santin (BSU), Nick Smith (BSU Alum), Emily Turner (BSU), Nykasia Williams (BSU)

Volunteers
Emily Badger, Sarah Bredar, Corrie Herron, Rachel Johnson, Mary Redman, and Iona Wagner

Organizations
Horizons Program at Saint Richards School
Indy Reads Books
LILLY Endowment
National Junior Honor Society at Fishers Junior High
Saint Florian Center Youth Leadership and Development Center
Teacher's Treasures
Westminster Neighborhood Services Youth Services Summer Program

Individuals
Kaitlyn Arford, Lauren Brown, Angela Jackson-Brown, Deb Carrell, Mallory Grantz
Deborah Mix, Carolyn Porzuczek, Joanne Prater, Kimberly Rowe, and Nicolette Zygmunt

www.ingramcontent.com/pod-product-compliance
Lightning Source LLC
LaVergne TN
LVHW081357060426
835510LV00016B/1880